50
YEARS OF SUNSHINE

GARY MORECAMBE

INTRODUCTION BY

JOAN MORECAMBE

CARLTON
BOOKS

CONTENTS

THIS IS A CARLTON BOOK

Design © Carlton Books Limited 2018
Text © Gary Morecambe 2018

This edition published in 2018

First published in 2013 by Carlton Books Limited, a division of
the Carlton Publishing Group, 20 Mortimer Street, London
W1T 3JW

Printed in Dubai

All rights reserved

A CIP catalogue for this book is available from the British Library

ISBN:978-1-78739-122-2

Introduction

BY JOAN MORECAMBE

Writing an extended introduction for a worthy book such as this gives one the chance to reflect, for the first time in my case, on the whole of one's life's experience; the journey that took me from Burma to London into show business, and into marriage with a unique, extraordinarily gifted comedian called Eric Morecambe. The memories seem like those of only yesterday, so quickly have the decades of that incredible journey flown by. It has been a journey experienced most intensely, and illuminated most thoroughly, through the remarkable story of Morecambe and Wise.

I recently paid a visit to the road in a small Surrey town where I was born. Ironically, the reason for going was because I now have a grandson living not just in the same town, but the same road!

As a baby, my early days were spent living with my parents and my brother Alan, just one year older than me, in the heart of London. My father was serving in the army and was based in Westminster, so that was where we had to make our home. It wasn't to be for long. When I was four, he was posted to Burma, and the whole family went with him. It broke my grandparents' hearts to see us sent so far away to a land they could never hope to visit.

It was an adventure to travel by ship all those miles, and in Burma we settled in a large bungalow with a big garden and a stream running by. It was an idyllic life, with a great social side to compensate for being so very far away from home. This was to last five years.

We arrived back in England on my tenth birthday. I can still picture the ship docking at the port and spotting my grandparents eagerly waiting on the dockside. In a sense, we were back where we started. We were living in London and spending most weekends with my grandparents in the country.

I had no memory of London from my early childhood, so it came as a big shock to me when confronted by it again. It was as though we had left a technicolour world behind and arrived in a grainy, somewhat drab black-and-white one.

My brother and I went to different schools, and began adjusting to this completely new way of life. Not that this lasted long, as the Second World War intervened. There was a moment of panic on the very first day of the announcement, because it was thought that London was about to be bombed by the Germans. It proved to be a false alarm. However, my brother and I were instantly evacuated and our parents were sent elsewhere, forced to abandon our London home with all its contents.

Arriving by train in Sussex along with so many other children, we found a group of cars waiting to take us all to a variety of houses as evacuees. My brother and I were placed with a couple on a farm where, for most of the time, we were separated. I certainly drew the short straw. The room where I slept had bare boards with no furniture other than a single bed. My one blanket was used on the ironing board during the day. The staple diet was boiled potatoes sometimes with a sausage thrown in, and also, occasionally, a very wet boiled apple pudding.

My mother was only able to see us briefly some weekends when her sister would drive her down by car. She would arrive with lots of goodies, none of which reached me. So eager was I not to cause my mother distress, that I didn't complain or say anything about the treatment I was getting from the people with whom I'd unfortunately been placed. The truth had to come out eventually about their meanness and general attitude. Of course, looking

back now, I can see it was no more than ignorance on their part. They didn't want extra mouths to feed and felt entitled to help themselves to whatever arrived that was intended for me – a sort of bonus payment, I suppose. But when my mother and my teacher saw my legs without the wool stockings that I usually wore, and now a mass of sores, my mother gave them a piece of her mind and I was whisked away to stay with my grandparents. I was soon enrolled at another school.

Before too long, my father was posted to Tidworth in Wiltshire. He was allocated a house, and the family was at last reunited. Tidworth was a large military camp housing thousands of servicemen. Weekly dances became a feature of the social life and this also created entertainment for the locals, particularly the young. Dances and concerts were laid on for the troops, many of whom were destined not to survive the fighting of D-Day. At the end of the war, my father, having been posted back to Burma, returned from the Far East deeply affected – traumatised – by his experiences out there. My brother had served briefly in the Airborne forces, having been called up when he reached the age of 18, and he became an officer. Post war, however, drastic changes were occurring for everyone.

Above Putting on their top hats, Eric and Ernie pose during a dance routine.

Opposite Can you see the join? One of Eric and Ernie's most famous gags involved Eric implying that Ernie wore a wig.

Below Eric's iconic spectacles.

For myself, nothing would be the same again. I was offered a free training course in London by a fashion agency and asked if I would like to become a fashion model. It sounded a glamorous career, but it wasn't. There were shortages of everything, and clothing remained obtainable only on ration coupons for years after the war had ended. At lunch breaks, I would dash out to my agents to see what else might have come up on their books. Eventually this led to my getting into show business.

In a sense, therefore, I was an accident of show business. I hadn't aimed to go into the business, despite having loved to act and sing at every opportunity from early childhood. And I'd taught myself to tap-dance. Eventually, I went on to become what used to be termed a "soubrette". This meant that one did little bits of everything, from speaking lines to singing a song, to setting up a gag for a comedian.

I was still very young when I arrived at what was then the Empire Theatre, Edinburgh, now the Festival Theatre. I saw that among the various variety acts performing that week was Morecambe and Wise. They were an up-and-coming double act that had begun building a solid reputation. I little realised then how this meeting would shape my future. Just in passing, I returned to the theatre in 2011 for the first time since meeting Eric there in 1952.

Eric and Ernie were full of enthusiasm and energy and loved show business. They were touring each week from town to town appearing in variety shows, as indeed was I, which is how it came to be that we were on the same bill in Edinburgh. As was the custom, the performers went to the theatre on a Monday morning for band call.

I had only just arrived and put my band parts down, bumping into Eric and Ernie who were doing likewise. Within a few hours, Eric told Ernie, "That's the girl I'm going to marry." Eric had taken such an immediate shine to me, that I found myself thinking, "Now hold on a minute – what's going on here?" Having said that, you only played each theatre for one week and then moved on to another, so there was no sense of being trapped in an environment; life was very much spent on the road.

Daytime life in the world of theatre could be quite boring, as you didn't turn up at the theatre until it was time for your make-up for the show in the evening. Invariably, to pass the time, most acts on the bill would go to the local cinema for the afternoon. Eric's persistence paid off, and we started meeting for a coffee in the mornings, then I would go to the cinema with both Eric and Ernie in the afternoon. It was quite ironic that, following on from Edinburgh, Eric and Ernie's next venue was my home town of Margate in Kent, and mine was to be Eric's home town of Morecambe in Lancashire. It worked out that they, and half of the Billy Cotton Band, stayed at my parents' hotel in Margate, and Eric arranged for me to stay with his parents in Morecambe.

I know it sounds very easy when reflecting back on those days but, without any doubt, I could see Morecambe and Wise had

tremendous potential. This was even before I got to know them well. They made friends very easily, and had the gift of making people laugh. There was something deeply infectious about their youthful enthusiasm. There are only so many comedians that you can say truly possess funny bones. "The Boys", as they were always referred to, were following on from the more stereotypical double acts of the era, who had been very successful in their time. I am not knocking them in any way, but Eric and Ernie were different. They were never stereotypical. Whenever I managed to catch a performance, they only ever did well.

It wasn't long before Eric and I were married in 1952, and a few weeks later, Ernie tied the knot with Doreen.

The years went by, their careers continued a meteoric rise both as stage and radio performers, and this coincided with the expansion of television which, after an up and down or two, became their natural home.

In the mid-1960s, Morecambe and Wise appeared regularly on Ed Sullivan's television show in America, and recorded in New York. They would do the show, then fly back a day or so later. Sullivan was an enormous mover and shaker in American television, so it was quite some privilege to be summoned back so many times. They were not seen enough over there, or for enough years (due to Eric's health deterioration), for them to build a new audience in America – the kind of audience they had spent

Top Eric and Ernie pretend to play their instruments while George Chisholm, renowned for his jazz music, really is playing the trombone.

Above Penelope Keith can't help but laugh during this sketch based on the story of Cyrano de Bergerac during their 1977 BBC Christmas show.

Opposite left A charming portrait of Ernie taken in the late 1980s or early 1990s.

Opposite right Eric had a lot of fun posing for this portrait by Richard Stone, which now hangs in the home that he shared with his wife Joan and their family.

so many years developing in Britain. Eric in particular was never interested in becoming a big hit in America, though Ernie felt differently.

Ernie and Doreen had chosen not to have a family, so as such had no real ties. He had this little bit of ambition to work in the United States, which stemmed from loving the glory days of old Hollywood. In reality, those days had long gone. And as Eric used to say, "Life's not Hollywood, it's Cricklewood." Eric's attitude was more pragmatic, less romantic. "It's taken a lifetime to become stars in our own country," he would say, "so why would we want to start all over again in another country?"

Before America, and before everything that television was going to bring to the boys, they hadn't been an immediate success

on television. As I mentioned, there had been downs as well as ups. The obvious down was their very first series for the BBC, titled Running Wild, and which was a theme of Victoria Wood's excellent biopic of their early years Eric and Ernie. They had no idea at the time how much media interest this first series of theirs was going to attract. The papers slated them, and it hurt that they were working in a new medium where they had to do as they were told by "the experts!"

All their scripts were written for them, and were dated in style with no new, fresh ideas. After that painful experience, they held back from accepting any more television, but eventually appeared on The Winifred Atwell Show, which happened to be the same day that I was in a nursing home giving birth to the author of this book, my son, Gary. He was our second child following on two and a half years after our daughter, Gail, was born.

As well as television series and Sullivan show appearances, the Sixties also gave the boys three film outings for the Rank Organisation. They really enjoyed making the films, but one cannot pretend they were classics, though they enjoy a cult following today.

It's the immense popularity and success of their television shows that gave them their entertainment immortality. Long gone were the variety theatre tours, and unless you could adapt to the demands of television your career was as good as over.

At the end of filming a television show, when the audience had left the building, Eric would stay behind to unwind. He liked to relax in the dressing room with the artistes who had appeared as guests on that particular show. Ernie never felt that compulsion to stick around afterwards, and he and Doreen would dash off almost immediately. I always watched each show with the audience and would meet up with everyone in the dressing room afterwards. When we finally arrived home, Eric would have a bite to eat and not go to bed for ages. Not until he was more relaxed.

When Eric had his near-fatal first heart attack, I think he felt he wanted to go back to work, but that he needed to give it a good amount of time before he actually did. In fact, he went back sooner than he had intended because he felt so well!

Eric was a nervous smoker, but gave up cigarettes the moment he was ill and never had another one again. He took to smoking a pipe, which in a way became his dummy. His pipe stems were chewed up quite regularly, particularly when he puffed away at a Luton football match, and I think it was something he not only enjoyed, but also it made easier the task of giving up the cigarettes for good.

The BBC deserves a lot of credit, not just for their patience during the period of Eric's recuperation from his illness, but always in terms of production values. No expense was ever spared, and such wonderful guests were encouraged to appear on their shows. Bill Cotton Junior (then Head of Light Entertainment at the BBC) gave so much support after Eric's illness. He agreed to extra rehearsal time so that they weren't running to such

a frantic schedule as before. The boys were also given longer shows, all pre-recorded and not recorded as live. This all made a great difference to Eric, particularly with the Christmas shows. They would still expend all their energies on the dance numbers, which was very much expected by their fans, but at least now they had the time they needed to work on the routines which, until Eric had been seriously ill, had never previously been a part of the work-rest equation.

If Eric had eventually retired, he would never have been bored. He would say that his hobby was hobbies. He took up bird watching and writing books, and fishing had been his main interest since early childhood when he used to fish with his dad in Morecambe Bay. He loved photography, music and reading. No shortage of things to occupy him.

No matter what happened during his life, Eric never lost his quick wit and could never resist giving an off-the-cuff response. But he did have a serious side and became much more philosophical in nature as the years wore on. Having had such a limited education, teaming up on the road with Ernie from around the age of 13, he became acutely aware that he needed to be able to do more than read and write. This was why he became such an avid reader. Even when he was a young man on the road touring, every train journey meant another book was devoured.

Eric never became big-headed. He needed the stability of a wife and home, and was devoted to his family. He regretted that work kept him away from home a lot when the children were young,

but he used to say, "The reason I work is for you and the family."

We weren't great partygoers. We liked to have friends to the house for dinner and to go to their homes. When we were at large functions, which were nearly always charity events, Eric just loved meeting up with other showbiz friends, particularly comedians. Were he alive today, he would have bought every available gimmick on the market, and he would have loved the Internet. He would have spent hours surfing early show business sites about old acts and theatres long-gone.

Along with Ernie, Eric was immensely proud of receiving an OBE from HM the Queen. It was a great moment in their lives, an affirmation of their immense achievement at having risen from humble beginnings to the top of their profession. Eric was also proud of receiving a doctorate from the University of Lancaster, the city of his birth. His proudest moment, however, was having his two children, Gail and Gary, who were later joined by Steven, whom we adopted as a four-year-old.

The public still has nostalgia for Eric and Ernie, and after all these years their shows are continually repeated, continually reviewed and always loved. Eric was a genius and a lovely man. He died far too young, and left a gap in my life which will never be filled. But he also left me with some truly wonderful memories.

**Joan Morecambe,
Harpenden, 2013**

CHAPTER 1

When Eric met Ernie

John Eric Bartholomew, to give Eric Morecambe his real name just for one moment, made his first appearance in Buxton Road, Morecambe on 14 May 1926. His parents, Sadie and George, were having some emergency damage repairs to their council house at number 48 during the final stages of her pregnancy, so Eric was, in fact, born a few doors down at their neighbours' house.

Far left A young Ernie on the fast track to child stardom.

Left A young Eric on the slow track to future stardom.

Above Eric and his parents moved to 43 Christie Avenue not long after his birth. Eric always loved the fact he could watch Morecambe FC play their matches from his bedroom window at their former ground, Christie Park. Well, half the match... there was a stand blocking part of the pitch!

A little unusually for the era into which he was born, he was an only child. This gave rise to the forging of a close, lifelong bond with his parents – a kind of "us against the big wide world" attitude.

Sadie, who would be instrumental in forming the Morecambe and Wise double act in years to come, was an intelligent, well-read woman, someone who struck you as being more than the sum of her given parts; certainly someone who rose above all the circumstances with which life presented her. As for many, living in the north of England pre-Second World War, surviving on nothing more than the man of the house was able to bring in, was never an obvious conduit for greater expectations. Indeed, the whole ambience of that era, described to me in detail when I was a child, made me – makes me – feel that Dickens might have penned their lives.

Sadie was a motivator, not a pushy mother, not someone trying to claim a share of the glory by encouraging her son towards the bright lights of show business. Sometimes, in books, articles and film, she is presented as a Mrs Worthington figure, whom Noel Coward implored not to put her daughter on the stage. It makes

for a more exciting story, of course, but is an entirely erroneous presentation of a woman whose only real ambition was for her son to better his lot in life. Recognising a spark of talent in him at an early age, she encouraged him to take the initiative and turn his talent into a life-changing advantage.

Showbusiness, therefore, became a natural choice for the young Eric, and he proved very able when it came to winning local talent shows. Once his talent and aptitude were recognised, and he showed no nerves or fear of performing (though a lot of embarrassment during the early days when his mother encouraged him to wear outlandish outfits), Sadie took that as her queue to urge him ever onwards. And she had to do so, because, as my father once told me himself, "If she hadn't, I wouldn't have done anything! I was intrinsically lazy."

George Bartholomew worked for the Morecambe Corporation (Council), labouring on myriad jobs, from road repairs to digging ditches, eventually spending much of his time erecting scaffolding and preparing stalls for the Lancaster market. George was Sadie's opposite, a man who delighted in the simplicity of life and sought nothing to add to it, because his life needed no additions or adornments. He had his fishing; he had his Heath Robinson bird traps in the garden: he could whistle and ballroom dance; he owned a bicycle and a Frank Spencer-style cap – what more did he need?

As Eric grew older, the fact that George could be so relaxed and untroubled, while Eric needed constantly to be on the go would sometimes become a small bone of contention between them. Eric more closely resembled his mother, although he may have lacked her serene calmness under pressure, a slow-starter who became a goal-chaser. Eric was also an only child, bereft of sibling rivalry and confident in the assumption that anything passing through the family was his by entitlement.

While the Bartholomews were living out their everyday life, with its occasional, then more frequent, forays into amateur showbusiness, Ernest Wiseman was doing likewise in his native Yorkshire. Born six months earlier than the man who would one day become so close to him that the outside world would view them as almost one life form, Ernie was brought up in East Ardsley, which is between Wakefield and Leeds. Ernie's father, Harry, was a railway porter and, as with Sadie and George Bartholomew, Harry and Connie Wiseman had been the attraction of opposites.

Connie came from a "well-to-do family", as it was charmingly called back in the day. Harry was considered far beneath her. Connie's father cut her out of his will for going against his wishes and marrying Harry. Ernie reflected on this time, "All she left home with was the piano she had saved so hard for as a young woman."

While Eric had clearly gravitated towards his mother's influence, Ernie was more remote from his parents with a different, individualistic approach to the way his life would pan out. Ernie had four siblings – a lot of mouths for Connie to feed, especially when funds were in short supply in the Wiseman household.

Harry's own father had toured Northern working men's clubs as a singer and Harry followed him, becoming well established on the circuit by the time of Ernie's birth. Ernie's bubbling

Above Eric's early solo act. It consisted mostly of a few dance moves, an ill-fitting costume which embarrassed him no end (see the caricature, left) a song called "I'm Not All There!" and a wooden lollipop. The lollipop he is holding was a present from Sadie for doing well in a talent competition.

Far left Sadie in thoughtful mood. Everything she did, she did for Eric and, later, for Eric and Ernie.

Opposite Jack Hylton, the impresario who began both Ernie and, later, Eric's career.

personality and eagerness to join his father in the show business fraternity of the day soon had the two performing together as "Bert Carson and His Little Wonder".

Ernie still kept up with his education, something he endured rather than enjoyed. This was similar to his one-day partner's approach to classroom learning, though in Eric's case his absences eventually far outweighed his attendances. Eric Bartholomew – the John had almost immediately been discarded for a reason no one ever clearly made known – was not only allowing his attendances in lessons to slip, but was often found on the school premises, "Smoking anything I could ignite," as he confessed many years later, not without a little pride.

Eric had a clear appreciation and understanding of his mother and how her brain ticked and what inspired her. He knew that her threats in regard to his lack of educational motivation were mostly idle ones. He knew that she saw he had a talent and felt as strongly as he that he needed to get into full-time showbusiness employment as soon as possible in order to start competing with the other young entertainers and would-be stars of tomorrow.

For a few years the Bradford *Telegraph and Argus* had staged an annual charity show at the Alhambra Theatre in Bradford with the unlikely, and politically incorrect in today's society, name of "The Nignog Revue". It featured child acts, and Ernie joined the troupe in 1936, appearing in three of these revues.

In 1938, the impresario Bryan Michie was touring the north of England looking for juvenile talent for a revue. Ernie had an audition with Michie, and was later contacted by bandleader Jack Hylton, who had been given the nod by Michie about the talented young Ernest Wiseman. Ernie did a very good Chaplin impression among other routines involving dance and song and jokes.

A rags-to-riches journey – or something along those lines – was about to begin for Ernie, as Hylton summoned him to audition for his show, *Band Waggon*, which was playing in Shaftesbury Avenue, in London's West End. Hylton was very impressed, and young Ernie found himself contracted to Hylton for three years.

While the railway porter's son was now a West End success in the making, it meant the demise of his faltering act with his father Harry. Hylton made it fairly clear to Harry that he was surplus to requirements and Harry took the train back to Leeds on his own.

Ernie was 13 years of age, but would never

live at home again, such were the life-changes that had now been set in motion. It would be many years before Ernie would begin to understand how Harry never quite came to terms with their separation. Every plaudit that Ernie enjoyed in the national press must have been a strange concoction of pride and pain to Harry.

While Ernie was on his surprisingly short journey from obscurity to child stardom, Eric was reluctantly undergoing music and dance lessons, which his mother was financing through a tearoom waitressing job and work for the Central Pier Theatre on Morecambe Bay.

"I didn't want to do them; simple as that," said Eric of these enforced lessons. "I never liked the lessons and I'd have much preferred to have spent my time kicking a ball around with my mates."

All of that is absolutely true, as I found out when I was privileged to catch up with some of those "mates" from his youth while researching a book in 2008. They described a solemn, embarrassed, young Eric bidding them farewell from their street football matches in Christie Avenue – a daily event – as he went

home to change into his top hat and tails to attend his dance lessons. Much mirth and jibing would greet his reappearance, and a poetic picture was painted of this melancholic lad lumbering off, wearing exactly the kind of costume that he would one day wear week-in, week-out to the delight of up to 27 million television viewers.

Though Eric's most influential role models were initially Abbott and Costello and later Laurel and Hardy – which was the same with Ernie – his first comedy hero was Lancashire star George Formby. Eric emulated his style, strumming a ukulele and wearing an ill-fitting costume, singing the Ella Shields number "I'm Not All There". It was such a performance that won Eric a competition in Hoylake, the prize for which was an audition before Jack Hylton.

Fate was definitely taking a hand in proceedings. Eric travelled with his mother to a cinema in Manchester, and Jack Hylton was not the only person present at the audition. Sitting next to him was his young protégé, Ernie Wise (as he had now become known). This, however, was not destined to be a landmark meeting of two future giants of British entertainment. One or two meaningful stares were all they managed.

Ernie was deeply impressed by Eric's act, and that unnerved him somewhat as his status as Hylton's rising young star had, up to that point, been unassailable. "Eric took to the stage and went into a number called 'I'm Not All There'," recalled Ernie. "This he followed with a very polished impression of Flanagan and Allen. How the hell he did it, I don't know! He played each character separately but somehow wove them together in such a way that we were convinced there were two people up there on stage."

After the audition, Hylton expressed interest and said he might well be in touch. As the weeks passed by there came no word from Hylton's office, bringing both Sadie and Eric to the conclusion that Hylton wasn't really interested in Eric. Then, three months later, Sadie received a telegram from Hylton asking if Eric would appear at the Nottingham Empire as one of Bryan

Michie's discoveries in the touring show, *Youth Takes a Bow*.

"My mother was expected to join me as chaperone on the tour," said Eric, "and my salary was to be five pounds a week plus travelling expenses."

A couple of months into the run, Eric heard a rumour circulating that Ernie Wise would be joining them at Swansea. By now, not only had Ernie starred with Arthur Askey in *Band Waggon*, but as a result of this triumph he had also made several radio broadcasts for the BBC.

"Even before I'd won that contest at Hoylake, I knew who Ernie Wise was," recalled Eric. "I can remember listening to him and a girl called Mary Naylor on the radio with Arthur Askey and 'Stinker' Murdoch.

"Ernie was taller than me in those days. And he was in long trousers. He joined the train at Crewe, but I didn't meet him until

somebody's mother introduced him to my mother while I was there. He said, 'Hi!' in a breezy fashion and bounced off. I used to watch him on stage, and he was good. He could do a good tap-dance and he looked so assured. But I thought he was a big-head."

In fact, Ernie's cockiness at this time was masking homesickness following the initial euphoria of the *Band Waggon* success. Sadie instinctively picked up on it and took Ernie under her wing. "The three of us were inseparable," Ernie said many years later, when recounting the beginnings of his career.

Despite the bonding between the three – though Eric and Ernie were still somewhat suspicious of each other – to all intents and purposes, Ernie was without a chaperone, and had to make all his own travelling and accommodation arrangements. This he did with great success, until the show reached Oxford in 1940.

The phoney war was over and the city was crawling with troops. He quickly discovered there was not a room to be had. He walked from house to house knocking on doors and was on the verge of succumbing to panic when, by chance, he knocked on the digs where Sadie and Eric were happily settled.

Fate would play an enormous part in the Morecambe and Wise story, and the conversation overheard by Sadie from the stairway in Oxford was just one of those fortuitous occasions. She recognised Ernie's voice, just as the landlady apologetically had to turn him away from the already full house.

"We can't turn him away," Sadie said to Eric, and with much irony (bearing in mind the many bedroom sketches to follow decades later in the double act's repertoire), Eric and Ernie shared a bed!

There was no looking back after Oxford, and Eric and Ernie's double act evolved naturally out of the time spent on the road travelling together. The moment they became a definite duo was when they found themselves with *Youth Takes a Bow* in war-flattened Coventry following Hitler's blitz on the city.

Above Eric's first ukulele. Ukulele player George Formby was something of a hero to Eric.

Below Morecambe and Wise pictured sometime in the late 1940s or early 1950s. By now they were showcasing their double act regularly at theatres nationwide.

Opposite top left Eric and his parents, George and Sadie, play their ukuleles in 1932.

Because of the state of the city, they travelled daily to digs in Birmingham. The 20-odd miles each way by train were a desperately slow journey, frequently disrupted. The boys whiled away the time doing gags and impressions, which after a time began to grind Sadie down. Finally reaching breaking point, she suggested, "Look, instead of all this malarkey, why don't you put your brains to better use and try and do a double act of your own? All you need are a few fresh jokes and a song."

Said lightly by a woman whose endurance had been stretched, and who was currently separated from her husband while taking on the chaperoning of two young entertainment hopefuls on tour, it was advice nonetheless taken extremely seriously by the two mischief-makers themselves.

Within days, they had their first routines worked out – a few fast gags and a soft-shoe dance to "By the Light of the Silvery Moon". Though they had to concentrate on their solo spots, Bryan Michie allowed them the chance to add a double-act spot when they reached the Liverpool Empire in August 1941.

As far as Eric and Ernie were concerned, they were now a double act

Above The Liverpool Empire Theatre, where Eric and Ernie first appeared as a double act.

Below Eric and Ernie appearing in panto. This is the first photographic instance I have been able to trace of Eric messing around with his glasses in this fashion.

ready to launch themselves on audiences, and the solo spots would soon, no doubt, be dropped. But while the earliest of foundation stones were put in place, this wasn't going to be a moment that heralded the arrival of a wonderful new comedy team. That was a decade-and-a-half away. It was, however, the beginning of a life-long partnership and friendship that would take them on the most amazing journey through the next 43 years.

While the second half of their remarkable story would move through a whirlwind of glory and achievement, the first half was to be a more turgid and unremarkable affair, with moments of sheer despair.

For starters, Hitler was standing in their way!

When hearts are young
'Tis then the sun
Sheds forth its brightest rays,
May you be blest with happiness
O'er each and all thy days.

A Happy
Birthday

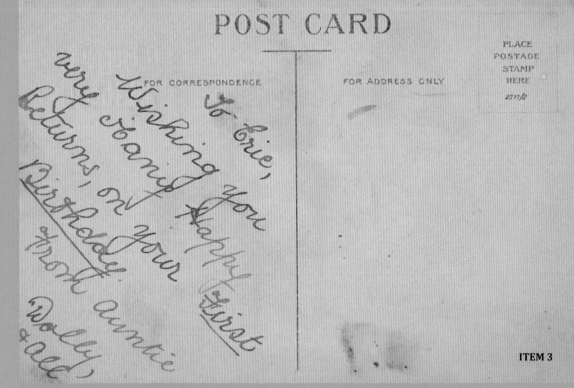

POST CARD

FOR CORRESPONDENCE

FOR ADDRESS ONLY

PLACE
POSTAGE
STAMP
HERE

To Eric,
Wishing you
very many happy
Returns, on your First
Birthday.
from auntie
"Dolly"
+ all

ITEM 3

Above and opposite Eric's first birthday
card from his Auntie Dolly, May 1926.

"Why don't you put your brains to better use and try and do a double act of your own?"

Sadie Bartholomew

CHAPTER 2

A Very Young Double Act

It was clear from the start – certainly to Michie and Hylton – that, however good Eric and Ernie's double act might be and however enthusiastic they were for it, their solo acts were what they were employed to do. This meant that any work on the double act was done privately, and in their free time.

Left In this early publicity shot from 1942, Eric is already working on the "poorly" look that would engender a sympathetic audience.

Most of the material they began regurgitating was stolen from other comedians, with a bit of Abbott and Costello thrown into the delivery. Indeed, Ernie came to claim in later years that they were in danger of *becoming* Abbott and Costello, with them even going so far as to use American accents during their spots, and Ernie addressing Eric as "Hey! Morecambe!"

The material was also very standard fare and not especially ground-breaking. Eric would walk onto the stage holding a fishing rod with an apple attached to the end of the line.

ERNIE: What are you doing?

ERIC: I'm fishing.

ERNIE: You don't go fishing with an apple. You fish with a worm.

ERIC: The worm's in the apple!

That example is representative of much of their material at this time, yet they did get a good response because the chemistry they shared, coupled with the fast pace at which they worked, was both engaging and impressive.

The double act was born at the Empire Theatre in Liverpool in August 1941, with Sadie watching her charges proudly from the wings. Hylton was watching, too, and liked what he saw despite the questionable material that they were using. He saw enough to convince him that they should do the act every night the

following week on the next stage of the tour in Glasgow.

There was one aspect of the act that held little appeal to any of them, and that was the name, Bartholomew and Wise. It was Adelaide Hall's husband, Bert Hicks, who recalled a friend of his in America adopting the name of the town from where he had originated. Henceforth, without further ado or public announcement, the boys became Morecambe and Wise.

Eric would often joke that they considered Morecambe and Leeds, "but it sounded like a cheap day return, so we dropped it", although nothing other than Morecambe and Wise was seriously considered.

Out on the road went the British equivalent of Abbott and Costello. If you ever see old footage of Abbott and Costello, it is hard at first to work out what Morecambe and Wise saw and later used in their performances that could possibly have worked for them. Clearly not the American accents.

Yet Eric and Ernie were much harder in their early years – they worked off much more standard cross-talk exchanges in the traditional funny-man-and-feed style of the day. And they were also far more slapstick in their performances. Comedian, writer and television presenter Paul Merton commented to me, "(Eric) was a great faller; an adroit physical comic, and you can't help but wonder if, in view of his love for some of the silent comedians,

global phenomenon that was Laurel and Hardy. Although it was wartime, Youth Takes a Bow toured until 1942, when box-office receipts began to drop. It was noticed by the whole troupe that Bryan Michie had seemed a little distracted for quite a while, and eventually the telegram came from Jack Hylton instructing him to close. For Eric and Ernie, it was no more than a new beginning in variety for their double act – or so they imagined.

Both of them felt that a move to London was the natural next step. There, they could find themselves a new agent and probably earn around £30–40 a week, according to Ernie. Sadie was unconvinced, pointing out that they had up to now been only employable as child discoveries. And also there was no work going. The truth was, as Sadie pointed out, "You are going to have to get real jobs for a time.'"

Eric returned to Morecambe taking a job in a razor blade factory. Ernie didn't return directly to Leeds, first wanting to try his luck in London to confirm for himself what Sadie was saying. He stayed with a family of Japanese acrobats, but variety in the capital truly was at a standstill, and soon he was packing his bags again to head for home.

Eric and Ernie kept in constant touch, Ernie often travelling to stay with the Bartholomews in Morecambe. They toured the area in search of local jobs, but always without a positive result. They then tried Leeds and its environs. Ernie was still fondly remembered from his days with his dad as Carson and Kid (as they became known), and this did lead to some work in both Leeds and nearby Bradford, but not enough either to sustain them or to develop the act.

Ernie made the remark in later years when reflecting on the tougher days while getting their act off the ground, that "the great

there was some inspiration from Buster Keaton there."

I would say that was very likely; Eric was a lifelong Keaton fan (and a Harold Lloyd fan), but it was Laurel and Hardy who would prove to be Eric and Ernie's most profound influence over the course of time. A gentle hero-worship for the two giants of Hollywood never left them, even after they became huge stars themselves.

"Our admiration for them centres on the seemingly effortless but utterly professional pace of their comedy," said Ernie, "and the way that the extremely funny juxtaposition of the skinny fellow and the fat one is matched by the difference in their natures: the hangdog pathos of Stan Laurel neatly contrasting with the bombastic dignity of Oliver Hardy."

Hardy himself described their act in an interview as two men who were very nice people but who never got anywhere, "because they are both so very dumb, but they don't know they are dumb." In the early 1980s, Eric said of Morecambe and Wise, "When we first had our own television series, Ernie was an idiot, but I was a bigger idiot." It's easy to make the link.

In the 1940s, it has to be said that there was little similarity between the fledgling double act of Morecambe and Wise and the

Above left Eric and Ernie were aware from the outset of the need to cultivate contrasting, but complementary, on-stage personalities.

Left The comedy of Stan Laurel and Oliver Hardy was a huge inspiration for Morecambe and Wise's fledgling double act.

thing about a double act is you're never alone in the cold, cold world. Problems are things you share".

Sensing disappointment and disillusionment, Sadie took the huge step of pushing them into the professional showbusiness arena by securing them digs in Mornington Crescent, London, and almost immediately finding them an agent. The agent, based in Charing Cross Road, suggested to the boys that they go to the Hippodrome where George Black was holding auditions for his new show, *Strike a New Note*.

George Black and his brother, Alfred, were big booking agents at this time and would later have a profound effect on Morecambe and Wise's meteoric rise via summer season shows in Blackpool. Ernie had previously met George Black while staying with Jack Hylton and his family. While this was advantageous, he didn't want to overplay that particular card, so when they auditioned, they gave Black their full act, now nine minutes long. Black hired them. They were little more than chorus boys and understudies and, as Eric observed many years later, "that cast must have been the healthiest ever to play a theatre!". Yet it was a great experience and *paid* work. Despite the war going on around them, *Strike a New Note* was a big success. It made Sid Field a big star, and the personalities who came to see the show were top drawer, including Jimmy Stewart, Clark Gable and Alfred Hitchcock.

Because of their lack of physical involvement in the production, Eric and Ernie had plenty of time on their hands to do other things. They made a foray into radio on the BBC's *Youth Must Have Its Fling*, and in the recording studio audience they were joined by some of their young fellow performers from *Strike* who were there to give them support. Just as the double act was beginning to move into positive territory, Ernie received his call-up papers summoning him to join the war effort.

Top left *Strike a New Note* – the show in which Eric and Ernie never got beyond the chorus line, but which gave them great kudos by association.

Top middle The boys with performer Jean Bamforth. She was known in these early days of their career as the third member of the double act.

Top right The pair are all smiles backstage at a show in 1948.

Above The bill for a June 1940 performance at the dreaded Glasgow Empire, where English performers were routinely devoured by Scottish audiences. Eric and Ernie (at the bottom of the bill) appear separately as this show pre-dates their first double act performance by 14 months.

CHAPTER 3

War Stops Play

The boys obviously appreciated that everyone was having to make sacrifices because of the war, but having to set their careers aside in order to do war work came as a devastating disappointment. Showbusiness had taken a grip, yet every positive step forward seemed to be followed by two negative steps back.

Left When war broke out and interrupted Eric and Ernie's burgeoning stage career, success suddenly seemed a long way off.

Ernie joined the Merchant Navy, working for the Gas, Light and Coke Company. His time was mostly spent on the rivers and estuaries shipping coal to Battersea Power Station from Newcastle and South Shields. Any time off he had was divided between visits to his family in Yorkshire and the Bartholomews in Lancashire. Though the Merchant Navy had suffered terrible losses during the war, Ernie did admit that by the time he joined up the worst was well behind them. The only enemy action he saw came from the daylight bombing raids over London.

Ernie was put in a "pool", which meant he was part of a reserve seamen unit on short-notice call. During long breaks between postings, Ernie continued to work in showbusiness, still doing spots for his mentor's right-hand man, Bryan Michie, who would engage him for a night or week, depending on his availability with the Merchant Navy. Michie, always able to make something useful out of a situation, happily presented Ernie during this period as "A boy from the brave Merchant Navy," and had him perform in his full naval uniform, ensuring patriotic fervour whenever he took to the stage.

Eric knew it wouldn't be too long before his own call-up papers arrived. He joined ENSA (Entertainments National Service Association) and became straight man to a Blackpool comic by the name of Gus Morris.

Eric developed a genuine fondness for Morris, who had been wounded during the First World War, his part in the conflict earning him the Military Medal. Eric would later describe the comedian as both kind and funny. Indeed, Eric often reflected on those times – brief as they were – as some of his fondest memories of life on the road. The raw uncertainty of everyday life at that time, matched with the fearlessness of youth, would leave him quite emotional when recalling these days to me decades later.

As the weeks and months passed by, Eric was gaining in experience all the time, particularly when playing the straight man. It would not be the last time in his career that he would take on that role.

Eric's papers arrived about six months after Ernie's, and he made what proved to be a bad decision by choosing to go down the mines as a Bevin Boy. Taking their name from Ernest Bevin, the then Minister of Labour and National Service, around 48,000 Bevin Boys worked in the coal mines during the war, replacing regular miners who had been conscripted into the armed forces. In recent years, the Bevin Boys have received belated recognition for their part in the war effort, but at the time, and for decades after, their efforts went virtually unnoticed and unappreciated.

Eric's father, George, suggested he tried for Accrington, where the Bartholomews had relatives. Almost immediately, Eric met a fellow entertainer called Gordon Jay who shared digs with him. Along with his brother, Bunny, they would become a stalwart pantomime double act for years to come, outlasting even the double act endeavours of Morecambe and Wise.

I interviewed Gordon in 2009, having discovered that we lived in the same neighbourhood after a chance encounter in

Shaftesbury High Street in Dorset. He told me, "We had one room with two iron bedsteads. Eric chose the bed by the window.

"We did a month together in digs... During the hours when we were back on our beds in the digs, we'd chat. Eric, I found, always wanted to talk about his mum and dad. He clearly thought the world of them: he worshipped them. He was always pondering on what they would be doing that day, and what they would have to eat...."

Gordon added, "I often wondered if the gang we were together with during the mining era ever realised who this young lad became. Probably not. It's not the most obvious connection, and he worked under a different name soon after the war."

Eric was not someone whom one would have described as being cut out for manual work, and grafting in the mines required constant physical effort. It was also dusty, claustrophobic and about a million miles from the world of entertainment to which he had become accustomed.

Arriving with A1 health, in just under a year he was re-classified as C3 with a touch of heart trouble and quickly discharged. Eric, much to his delight, found himself back home in Morecambe with his parents, where he would be able to recuperate (though he never made a full recovery) under the particularly close attentions of a loving and doting mother.

Eventually, Eric was back on his feet and soon returned to work at the razor blade factory. Meanwhile, Ernie was splitting his time between the Merchant Navy and the stage. Eric finished his run at the factory at about the same time that Ernie received his discharge papers. Purely by chance, Ernie found himself drifting down Regent Street in London's West End in no particular hurry, when he bumped into Sadie and Eric. If you were to drop such serendipity into a fictional tale, no reader would be able to suspend disbelief, yet this was precisely how the boys' first post-war meeting came about. Sadie, admirably adept at making good, quick decisions, suggested that Ernie join them in their digs at Clifton Gardens, Chiswick, which were owned by a Mrs Duer. Sadie, of course, had an ulterior motive. She wanted the boys to get back together and renew their double act, though Ernie had been quick to explain that he wanted to give his solo work some attention instead.

Ernie would later say of that chance meeting that he knew at once that inevitably he had to go along with what Sadie wanted, because you could never talk her out of something she had set her mind on. As her grandson, I would concur with that opinion. She had the knack of selling you her ideas so that you walked away feeling you must have made the best decision.

Sadie found work for the newly reformed double act pretty quickly. It would possibly be the strangest work of their long careers in entertainment, but it was something that would forever remain in their memories, bringing smiles to their faces whenever it was brought up in conversation.

Lord John Sanger's Circus and Variety Tour was one of the more innovative, if not plain bizarre, showbusiness ventures of the time. Sanger had bravely set out to combine two areas of entertainment under one roof – or canvas, to be completely correct. The tour was made in caravans, and a big top was erected at the designated site of each outdoors venue. It boasted a full range of entertainers, from clowns and novelty acts, to dancers, singers and comedians.

As Ernie put it, "It promised audiences the best of both worlds, but proved to be the lowest common denominator, looked down on by circus and variety people alike."

The audience came in one entrance and passed out through another in a continual stream (or so went the notion), with the troupe keeping up an almost non-stop performance. Seventeen shows on the first day, 24 on the second and 32 on the third and final day. Remarkable, but it didn't stop the show from closing, as many of these performances were staged for empty seats.

The black period of their career working together now set in. They returned to Mrs Duer's. Sadie was back in Morecambe much of the time now, if only to prove to George that he still had a wife!

Eric and Ernie chased work and various agents on a daily basis, but a year of unemployment passed, during which they barely got by. I have often thought that there is a play in this waiting to be written – the year Morecambe and Wise shared a flat, but never worked! There is something in their situation at this time that dovetails neatly with their BBC onscreen characters decades later.

The memory of being "child discoveries" was exactly that – a memory, and an increasingly distant one. They were young men, now in their twenties, and to have a future together they had to get on to the variety hall circuits in order show what they were able to do. But that was proving very difficult to achieve, as seemingly no one actually wanted them.

Opposite After the war was over and Eric and Ernie were returned to civilian life, they met each other purely by chance... walking down London's Regent Street.

Left Eric's make-up box, which still contains the pancake base that he used. He wrote notes on the inside of the lid for his act.

CHAPTER 4

Stars in the Making

The traditional entertainment of the variety halls had developed from tavern entertainment – halls added to the back of pubs – before blossoming and moving into independent theatres. Variety's golden age was during the Victorian era and it would slowly slip into terminal decline after the Second World War. It was already beginning to suffer when Eric and Ernie were first trying to get along in it, and had been since the 1930s as radio, film and, eventually, television came to dominate the entertainment industry, luring audiences away from the theatres.

Above The Walthamstow Palace Theatre, pictured in 1910. It was here, in 1948, that Eric and Ernie got their first post-war break.

Left Morecambe and Wise delivering classic variety hall schtick. It took them several years to make an impact on the circuit.

Although variety shows no longer exist in the way that they did when the theatres were booming, they haven't disappeared altogether. Britain's Got Talent is a direct link to those past times of novelty acts and entertainers performing in front of a live theatre audience, and stand-up comedians often tour the country with a small show of support acts on the bill.

Billing was the crucial thing for performers in variety. It directly related to their wages. "I don't want to be fourth or fifth on the bill," Ernie said. "I wouldn't like the loss of face. I don't subscribe to the old showbiz adage of being nice to people on the way up, because you'll see them on the way down. This business is all based on success; and if you're a failure on your way down, no one wants to know you."

It would take Morecambe and Wise until 1952 really to begin to make any kind of impact in variety shows. Those five years separating them from the bleak days at the welcoming home of Mrs Duer in Chiswick, five years spent climbing variety hall bills, was a very tough half-decade that would have defeated many other acts.

Money was unbearably tight in Chiswick. Eric was trying to survive on the two pounds a week sent to him by Sadie, and Ernie

was relying on his meagre savings. Adding to the stress of not being able to find work came the swift realisation that they were trapped in a "Catch-22" situation. No agent, no work – no work, no agent.

They found sporadic work by resorting to begging or bribing – sometimes both simultaneously – the booking manager of a theatre to put them on the bill. It was the only way they were going to tempt any agent along to see what they were about.

This more direct approach led to them winning themselves a week at the Walthamstow Palace in 1948. They were reluctantly billed as Morecambe and Wisdom to avoid confusion with another act on the bill called Vic Wise and Nita Lane, hilariously billed as "The Weak Guy and His Weakness"! The boys were not a success, and the management dropped them.

The Windmill, more famed for its nudes than true comedy, was their next port of call. Under the ownership of Vivian Van Damm – known affectionately throughout the entertainment industry as VD – the theatre introduced the boys to a series of somewhat suspect, chiefly male, audiences of the non-stop nude shows, called (as a play on the word "Vaudeville") "Revuedeville".

Despite the unlikely possibility of such a venue producing much

so soon was not funny back then. Van Damm, however, was a decent man and agreed to Ernie's request that they put an ad in *The Stage* (the industry's weekly oracle) to say that they were leaving the Windmill by mutual agreement. Ernie's reason for this was a plan he had to blitz all the London agents with complimentary tickets, paid for out of their own wages, in an effort for them to be seen performing before finding themselves unemployed again.

All this effort resulted in just one agent turning up to see their act. His name was Gordon Norval. Norval liked them and agreed to take them on. He had two show dates in the offing – at The Grand in Clapham and at the Kilburn Empire. The boys had been hoping for bigger dates than these, but in the circumstances they were delighted just to be getting more work. Norval was offering £20 a week, but for two spots. They hastily agreed and signed on the dotted line. Only afterwards did they realise to what they had committed.

After ten years of working together they had managed to run their routine to around 12 minutes. They had one week to come up with another ten minutes.

They worked constantly on new ideas, and seven days later, in 1949, it was the Clapham Empire that became the venue in which they were destined to try out their new material, all the fresh stuff being reserved for their second spot. They were given what have always been regarded as the two toughest spots on the bill – second in the first half, and second after the interval.

in the way of comedy, Van Damm introduced some great comic talent who would, like Eric and Ernie, become household names in just a few years. Among them were Tony Hancock, Dick Emery, Jimmy Edwards, Terry Scott, Harry Worth and Harry Secombe.

Bruce Forsyth spent a year at the Windmill Theatre and fared better than most – certainly better than Morecambe and Wise. Bruce found the challenge of unresponsive men in macs, as it were, a great way to sharpen his act and his interaction with an audience. "If somebody told you to do your act on the corner of Piccadilly Circus you'd just go on and do it, because you were tuned in to walking on and performing anywhere at any time," he told author William Cook.

Eric and Ernie auditioned for Van Damm, got a regular spot and, unlike the seven comics named above failed to raise a laugh from the dirty, scruffy audience that was simply hungry for the next nudes to appear. The nude shows were all very innocent by today's standards – lit in a way that made them more silhouettes than naked women, and required by law to remain statuesque throughout the performance.

Many years later, when Van Damm approached Morecambe and Wise to have their names engraved on a plaque to commemorate his list of successful comedians who had played at the Windmill, Ernie took great pleasure in reminding him that he had fired them!

Although funny many years later, being unemployed again

Above Working the pantomime season was standard fare for anyone wanting to carve out a career in showbusiness in the 1950s.

Right Vivian Van Damm, who ran London's famous Windmill Theatre and who both booked and quickly fired Morecambe and Wise.

Far right The Windmill Theatre was better known for its "Revuedeville" nude shows than its comedy.

Opposite Standing shoulder to shoulder. Being sacked from the Windmill was a huge blow but more prosperous times were looming.

Above left Eric's parents, George and Sadie, on the left, with relatives. It was a musical family.

Above right A youthful Eric and Ernie pose for a promotional photograph together.

Right Ernie (left) and Eric (second from the right on the righthand bench) in a 1954 *Babes in the Wood* production for Stan Stennett.

Below left Eric and Ernie with one of their own comic heroes, the northern comedian Albert Modley.

Below right Another scene from *Babes in the Wood*.

If they had hoped that the familiarity of their material in the first spot would give them confidence, they were soon very disappointed. They left the stage to the sound of their own footsteps.

But disaster turned into triumph, and Ernie said that it was probably the hurriedness of having to find material for the second spot while tucked away at Mrs Duer's that gave it that vitality. It also introduced something that would become familiar to many audiences in the ensuing months – their own interpretation of "The Woody Woodpecker Song".

The idea was that Ernie would tell Eric that he was going to teach him to sing a song in which he, Eric, had the most important part. Ernie emphasised that the success of the song was Eric coming in at the right time. A very simple idea, but beautifully set up for ensuing mayhem. Needless to say, Ernie's role in the song was everything, with Eric being reduced to no

more than the last five notes of each verse, those being Woody Woodpecker's cackling noise. From the unfortunate silence of their first spot, they now brought the house down.

Various managements spotted this "new" talent, and Nat Tennens booked them straight after – "act as seen" – for the Kilburn Empire.

They decided to reverse the order of their two spots; an intelligent move as the Woody Woodpecker song encouraged the audiences to laugh at the old material, too.

It was back to Clapham after Kilburn, and their return to Kilburn after that was as top of the bill. Gordon Norval became their full-time agent, and their earnings rose to £40 a week.

It was a long way from the days on the road with Lord John Sanger's Circus, but one member of that troupe had come back into Ernie Wise's life. Her name was Doreen Blythe. She had been one of four dancing girls on the ill-conceived tour and had maintained regular contact with Ernie. The two had begun to go steady, and I know that

GLASGOW Empire

Taken at
FINSBURY PARK EMPIRE
LONDON, N.4.
BY
Derek Grayson

Above a programme for a revue at the Regal Theatre in St Leonards in which Eric and Ernie performed in the early 1950s.

Above The ptorgamme for the production of Babes in the Wood with Stan Stennett, Freddie Sales et al at the Lyceum Theatre in Sheffield in 1953.

my father felt slightly out of it. He admitted he was very happy for them both but he would have loved to have had a girlfriend, too, someone who would care about him and vice versa. He just couldn't see that happening during this manic period of their working lives.

From Ernie and Doreen's perspective, having Eric tag along wherever they went was equally frustrating. In an interview a few years ago, Doreen mentioned that she would go to greet Ernie off a train, not having seen him for a long while, and suddenly Eric would appear a few yards behind. While Eric was aware he was a gooseberry in their reunions, it can't have made for much of a romantic interlude for Ernie and Doreen.

Meanwhile, back on the improving work front, with the woodpecker number working so well, they were less pressurised into coming up with new material, and more able to amend and rehearse the earlier stuff, with particular attention to delivery. What was clearly evident was that this flourish of success, courtesy of one number added to their repertoire, encouraged them to be much more relaxed and confident in how they came across. "It was all in a subtle change of emphasis or our facial expressions," Ernie explained, "and as we got better, we stopped pinching other comics' material and actually found the confidence to invent some routines for ourselves."

Not that true success had suddenly arrived. The really tough years were behind them, but the glory days were some way off. And success varied from performance to performance depending, as much as anything, on the audience.

The Glasgow Empire, for instance, was a no-go zone for English comedians. When they first tackled the Glasgow Empire, a very young Royal Navy lad, one day to become a film star called Sean Connery, was in the audience. Connery thought that they coped

dummy) during their television show, were two repeated comic moments shamelessly associated with the variety halls. The ventriloquist's doll became a staple of the touring Morecambe and Wise show in the early 1970s. And then you had the speciality acts, such as Wilson, Kepple and Betty, the Egyptian-styled dancers, which Eric and Ernie brought to television in their wonderful Anthony and Cleopatra sketch with actress-turned-MP Glenda Jackson.

Ernie was, without doubt, a driving force in their act during these early days of variety touring. Ernie didn't allow them to coast along and, had Eric been a solo act, that is precisely, by nature, what he would have allowed to happen.

Variety's decline was noticeable, but largely ignored in the 1950s when Eric and Ernie began to enjoy their working life. What remained impressive was the quality of the shows, the power of the bookers and the excellent running of the theatres by the likes of giants such as Moss Empires. Artistes still craved the best variety dates, and summer season and/or pantomime in locations such as Sheffield, Blackpool, Great Yarmouth and Bournemouth were as much an entertainment mecca for hopeful variety performers as Hollywood was to a budding film actor.

A variety tour entertainer of the day, who became a great lifelong friend of Eric and Ernie, was the comedian and singer Sir Harry Secombe. I talked with Harry some years ago, and it was clear that he had never lost his love for my father and Ernie and the sheer brilliance of their partnership. If ever during our conversation I referenced another double act, he would shake his head despairingly and say, "Pygmies!" A genuinely warm and caring man with easy charm and an engaging laugh, it is easy to understand how a young double act on the road would have gravitated towards him.

They first met Harry Secombe at the Croydon Empire, and later did panto season together in Coventry, a few photos of which still exist. "Many of us had been entertaining in the services," he recalled. "Mainly concert parties. And we had a different kind of humour to the civilian humour. And that's what we brought back after the war. The 'Goon' stuff, that basically (Spike) Milligan wrote, was all to lift comedy; to give it a different kind of feeling."

Sadie was by now a distant figure to the boys in terms of any involvement in their act, but she and George both kept abreast of their improving situation from home in Morecambe. In Victoria

very well under the circumstances as he recalled many years later on a James Bond set at Pinewood.

These years in variety are curious on two counts. First, it is easy to assume that Eric and Ernie were aiming for the top of the comedy tree. Not so. Eric told me he would have been happier had they remained second on the bill – in other words, highly regarded but with none of the stress of carrying the production on the back of their names. I'm sure this is why he reflected so positively on this more carefree period of his working life when discussing it with us, his children, in later years. You could really see his eyes light up and his voice become charged with excitement from the memories of those touring days.

Also, it is too easy to assume that Morecambe and Wise were a variety act that successfully transferred to television. In a sense that is absolutely what they were, but they continually developed into more than the original sum of their parts. As comedian and writer Ben Elton said, "Their success had nothing to do with variety. It was simply because they were the best comedy act in living memory and, in particular, a stunning live act."

I know that Eric liked to use old moments from variety routines in their huge BBC television shows – a sort of friendly nod and thank-you, perhaps, for giving them the leg up the showbiz ladder. Certainly the paper bag gag, a great comic idea that Eric stole from a clown he knew, and bringing on Oggy (the giant ventriloquist's

Wood's excellent film of Morecambe and Wise's early years, simply titled *Eric and Ernie*, Sadie is portrayed as barely able to come to terms with no longer being needed on the road with "her boys", and leaves them on a station platform with tears of sadness running down her cheeks as the train chuffs its way back home. Victoria had a film to make, and quite understandably chose to use this dramatic imagery. The truth was a little more prosaic. Sadie was delighted when Ernie took greater charge of their affairs and she could at long last get back to George, who might have been forgiven "for thinking he'd become a widower" as Sadie herself worded it.

But another massive development was just around the corner for Eric and Ernie. In 1952, in her usual, frank way, Sadie directly asked Ernie when he and Doreen were to get married. "Oh, some time, I expect," came his vague response. He went on to say that he would wait until Eric found someone and got married, because he didn't want to give away half his pay packet to a woman and have Eric laughing in the background.

Within a year of that conversation, both men were married.

Morecambe and Wise were booked to play the Edinburgh Empire (now the Festival theatre) in June 1952. A former model and dancer who had turned to showbusiness, Joan Bartlett, from Margate, Kent, was on the same show as a replacement for another dancer who had been taken ill with appendicitis.

Joan had heard of Morecambe and Wise, but never seen them. As a little more accurately covered in Victoria Wood's film of their early lives (though the venue they chose for the film was Glasgow), Eric never relented in his pursuit of my mother, Joan.

"It is true," she told me. "Eric wanted to mount a plaque outside the theatre stating, 'Where Eric Morecambe Fell, 1952.'"

My mother added, "Sadie realised that when Eric was no longer a child, her role as mother, minder and manager was coming to an end. First it was Ernie who took on the responsibility, then it was me."

And she also said, "From the very beginning, Eric told me he had to have a woman in his life. And by 1952, he had reached a stage where he was very restless."

Eric and Joan married on 11 December, 1952. Almost in shocked response, just over one month later, Ernie and Doreen were married. Eric and Ernie were each other's best man.

Doreen had given up dancing some while ago, and was now running a dancing school, which was the main reason they cited for their decision to choose not to have children. All the children she had encountered through school had proved more than enough for a lifetime.

"When we first met, Doreen thought I was pushy and obnoxious," said Ernie, "dedicated only to performing and making money. And I suppose I was. But Doreen has been the only one for me."

Once both men were married, their lives would become more adult, more separated by the two natural halves of working and private life. Suddenly they were no longer jaunty former child performers made good; they were mature men with responsibilities and permanent, separate addresses.

They made an immediate decision to keep their working and personal lives separate to protect their close friendship and partnership. Both men separately claimed that it was that significant decision which enabled them to consistently perform together for the next 32 years – from the time they were married right up to Eric's death.

Meanwhile, the variety tours continued. But dark clouds were forming, and Eric and Ernie were both alert to their arrival. Just prior to, and in anticipation of, HM the Queen's coronation in June 1953, many families started acquiring television sets for their homes. It wasn't to prove a passing fad. Quite the opposite, it is now regarded as the jump-point of mass television viewing, and certainly sounded the death knell for the variety tours and many of their performers.

To.
Eric and Joan.
will love.
Ernie and Doreen.
xxxx 1953.

Above A souvenir card of their wedding which Ernie and
his wife, Doreen, sent to Eric and Joan as a memento of their
marriage in 1953.

"Their success had nothing to do with variety. It was simply because they were the best comedy act in living memory."

Ben Elton

CHAPTER 5

Through the Cloud Comes Sunshine

Nineteen fifty-three was a watershed year for Morecambe and Wise. As television began its at first slow but ultimately unstoppable assault on people's homes, Eric and Ernie would have the chance to become a part of the new entertainment it was bringing into the living room.

Prior to that, what made 1953 memorable was two-fold. On a personal level, Eric became father to a daughter, Gail – my big sister! Secondly, Eric and Ernie rekindled their acquaintance with George and Alfred Black, George fondly remembering their involvement (for what it was) in 1943's *Strike A New Note* show.

George and Alfred Black were big bookers in the fifties, just as they had been back in the 1940s, and held the crown jewels of variety entertainment – spots in summer season at Blackpool. Blackpool was beyond all other venues – the centre of the British holiday market, before Spain and its neighbours began to lure away its visitors with the promise of guaranteed sunshine.

In the mid-1800s, Blackpool was a very small town with less than a thousand inhabitants. Being built on the water's edge, however, it soon began to develop as a seaside resort for visitors escaping the monotony of industrial cities. The sight of the Blackpool tower, constructed in 1893 just a few years after the notably similar-looking Eiffel Tower in Paris, must have been a surreal, magical vision for the earliest visitors to the developing resort.

Blackpool soon built a reputation as the place to be when you had some hard-earned holiday time and just as soon had three piers, each with its own theatre. With the improvements in rail and coach travel, as well as the arrival of affordable cars for private motoring, in the 1950s Blackpool saw its population reach over the million mark at the height of the summer season.

Eric and Ernie enjoyed all their theatre seasons, summer and winter, before television gradually pulled them away from that line of work. But Blackpool had a special camaraderie; all the other pros would be there and you would constantly be bumping into them, sharing some banter. The feeling was that all was well with the world when you were working Blackpool. The audiences were responsive, promoting this wonderful feeling of well-being, an understanding that you should be working nowhere else during the summer months in Britain other than this one specific seaside resort.

Eric and Ernie were at the Winter Gardens, and I find it interesting to note that the Beverley Sisters were on the bill at the nearby Central Pier. Possibly no coincidence then that eight years

later they would become weekly regulars on the Morecambe and Wise ATV show.

Eric and Ernie, like all the acts who earned themselves a Blackpool season, did very well. Just saying that you did summer season in Blackpool put you in a good light, and it was undoubtedly this first outing that laid the true foundation stones of what would be a long and successful career. Blackpool was scrutinised by all those in the business; they would never go unnoticed again.

Of course, that didn't mean they were suddenly stars. What it meant was that for the first time in their showbusiness lives they had something approaching security in their work.

"By 1954," said Eric, "we were a success in variety and radio. We were beginning to make an impact. The only accurate barometer of success in showbusiness is the money you make, and we were making it."

It was no surprise that by the end of their first run in Blackpool in '53, they had drawn the attention of television, specifically the BBC. A producer called Ronnie Waldman, who was then Head of BBC Light Entertainment, approached them. He offered them their own series – *Running Wild*. It was destined for disaster and

Top Eric strums a tune. Sadie fostered a musicality in Eric during his childhood, apparently encouraging his learning of the piano, clarinet, trumpet, euphonium, accordion and mandolin!

Above Showbiz football XI. Eric (far left) is joined by Stan Stennett (front row left), with his son Roger, who is still in regular contact with me.

Opposite A still from the Beatles' appearance on the Morecambe and Wise ATV show in 1963. Ringo is out of shot… keeping the beat!

theoretically should have set Morecambe and Wise back years, if not ended their career for good. Their friend, the singer Alma Cogan, would be the only triumphant figure from the series.

The biggest problem for Morecambe and Wise was that they were new to the television game. They weren't allowed to use their own ideas or material. The material they were given was already dated, and just not them in content. Eric and Ernie quickly came to understand that the BBC was not overwhelmed with the idea of Morecambe and Wise fronting Running Wild, and this before the cameras had even begun to roll. They castigated Waldman for employing comedians with northern accents. It seems extraordinary today, but back then the BBC mostly was only recruiting white upper-middle-class types who spoke public school English. The north-south divide was still very strong. The witch-hunt theory is something I have mentioned many times down the decades regarding this series. At the time, Ernie remarked, "We're northern, and you can't win if you're northern." Happily, we live in a time where any actor/comic/

presenter can come from any part of the globe and be on prime-time television.

It cannot be denied that Morecambe and Wise were fundamentally a northern comedy act, but they had worked venues deep in the south of England and had gone down very successfully with audiences at theatres such as the Chiswick and Brixton Empires. Ronnie Waldman clearly appreciated this, and that is why he was so supportive. But with the other executives

Above Another Christmas meant another pantomime season – this time in Sheffield.

Opposite A standard fare publicity still. Such contrived photo opportunities permeated their careers from beginning to end. The press always wanted them to "do something funny".

Right and above Panto and summer season were the basis of Morecambe and Wise's career from the early days until Eric's heart attack in 1968.

Below and opposite The programme for the "Spring Show" at the Palace Theatre in Manchester in 1961. It was subtitled "A Gay Springtime Spectacular". Well, what else could one call a Spring show!

LES CHARLIVELS

The Charlivels are probably one of the best known speciality acts in the world to-day. Their acrobatics, music and comedy are so well blended that the boys have been featured in most of the famous theatres and night-spots in the world. In Britain, for instance, they have been featured at the London Palladium, and were one of the starring attractions at the opening of London's most luxurious theatre-restaurant, "The Talk of the Town".

Their versatility stems from the fact that the boys are the sons of the renowned Spanish circus clown, Charlie Rivel, who brought them up to be masters of the theatrical arts.

KAZBEK & ZARI

. . . present one of the most thrilling speciality acts on the stage to-day. The curling whip used with such dexterity by Kazbek has audiences gasping.

Freddie FRINTON

. . . can claim nationwide fame for his rendering of "Sugar in the Morning"—the song first made famous by Alma Cogan. His many appearances in television's "Arthur Haynes Show" have established him as the king of comedy drunks.

After this Manchester season, he commences work on a comedy film at Pinewood.

MORECAMBE and WISE

Morecambe (the one with the glasses) actually hails from the famous resort—his real name is Bartholomew; Wise, whose real name is Wiseman, comes from Leeds. They first teamed up in 1940 after Eric's mother, suggested that they would make a good comedy act.

Eric Morecambe, married with a boy and a girl, is just about to move into a spanking new house at Harpenden. Ernie Wise, who is also married, lives in an elegant home in Peterborough.

5 Dallas Boys

The average age of this dynamic group is only 23½. It comprises Stan Jones, Leon Fisk, Bob Wragg, Joe Smith and Nicky Clarke. The first four hail from Leicester, the latter is a Londoner.

All five readily analyse themselves thus: Joe—good natured and easy going; Stan and Leon—forceful and outspoken; Nicky — friendly and absent-minded and Bob — quiet and moody.

Their first break came after winning a talent contest and this led to a TV series with Petula Clark. Since then they have chalked up many recordings and television appearances.

Rosemary SQUIRES

... who was born in Bristol, has been singing professionally for 13 years and is now one of our busiest female stars.

Rosemary's success stems from the time she had plastic surgery just over two years ago. She was given a new nose and from then on, her luck seemed to change and contracts flowed in.

There has always been show business in the Squires family for Rosemary's mother was a soubrette, and her aunt starred in silent films. Before she became an entertainer, Rosemary worked in an antique bookshop, but she had to leave because of her inability to give the correct change!

Billy DAINTY

... was born in Dudley and began his career at the age of 12 as the only boy in a juvenile troupe of girls. Looking back on this, Billy admits that he could kick himself for being a backward boy!

His hobbies are golf, fishing and travelling. His most unusual memory of fishing was the time he caught an octopus at Babbacombe. His friend David Nixon sent him a telegram; "Teach it to play the bagpipes and get it in the act!"

LESLIE A. MACDONNELL presents S.H. NEWSOME'S SPRING SHOW — A Gay Springtime Spectacular

Directed by JOAN DAVIS

First performance: Tuesday, April 18th, 1961

OVERTURE   "SPRING IS HERE"
LARRY MACKLIN & THE PALACE MUSIC MEN

"SPRING IS IN THE AIR"
THE DEBONNAIRES
introduce
A Shower of Lovelies   ..   ..   THE DEBUTANTES
Singing in the Rain   ..   ..   ..   ROSEMARY SQUIRES
Those April Fools   ..   ..   ..   MORECAMBE & WISE
A Breath of Springtime   ..   ..   ..   FREDDIE FRINTON
The Pipes of Pan   ..   ..   BILLY DAINTY
And that Exciting Touch of Spring
ALMA COGAN

THE FUN CONTINUES
ALMA and the BOYS

TALENTED TUMBLING
THE THREE GHEZZIS

SONG TIME
ROSEMARY SQUIRES

GOING MAD—COMING?
BILLY DAINTY

SPRING KICKING
THE DEBUTANTES

YOU'RE ONLY YOUNG ONCE
MORECAMBE & WISE

A BIT OF EVERYTHING (*Scenery by Tod Kingman. Costumes by R. St. John Roper*)
by Those International Stars
THE CHARLIVELS

INTERMISSION

"LIGHT AS A FEATHER"
THE DEBONNAIRES and the DEBUTANTES

GUESS WHO'S WHO
Introducing Three Surprising Guest Stars

THE FABULOUS FIVE
THE DALLAS BOYS

DINNER FOR ONE
The Butler   ..   ..   FREDDIE FRINTON
Her Ladyship ..   ..   MAY WARDEN

HE'S HERE AGAIN
BILLY DAINTY

NIGHT IN THE CASBAH
The Sailors ..   ..   THE DEBONAIRES
The Slave Dancers ..   ..   THE DEBUTANTES
featuring
KAZBEK & ZARI

FOOLING AROUND
MORECAMBE & WISE

STAR TIME   (*Decor by Alec Shanks*)
ALMA COGAN
with STAN FOSTER at the Piano

FINALE
THE ENTIRE COMPANY

THE DEBONNAIRES . . .
Bob Hargreaves, George Lucas, Ron Lucas, Tony Marlowe, Peter Murray, John Webster.

THE DEBUTANTES . . .
Patricia Squibb, Christine Carroll, Christine Chapman, Mary Cochrane, Marjorie Edwards, Pat Fudge, Pamela Hill, Margaret Jenkins, Elsie Langley, Joan Langley, Margaret McDermott, Julie Pickles, Maureen Robins, Susie Smith, Lesley Vipond, Christine Walhead.

THE PALACE MUSIC MEN with LARRY MACKLIN

Scenery constructed in the Coventry Theatre Workshops. Shoes and tights by Anello & Davide.
Wigs by Wig Creations Ltd. Wardrobe care by WHITE TIDE.
Hoovermatic Washing Machine used in wardrobe by Hoover Ltd., Perivale, Middlesex.
S. H. Newsome gratefully acknowledges the assistance of Moss' Empires Production Department by kind permission of Leslie A. Macdonnell.

For Newson Productions Ltd.
Company and Stage Manager   ..   ..   Douglas Freear
Deputy Stage Manager   ..   ..   ..   Donald Auty
Master Carpenter   ..   ..   ..   Wilfred Hurworth
Wardrobe Mistress   ..   ..   ..   Mrs. Gertrude Jackson
Chief of Wardrobe Department   ..   ..   Mrs. Mabel Mason
Publicity Manager   ..   ..   ..   T. W. Willis

FULLY LICENSED BARS IN STALLS, GRAND CIRCLE & UPPER CIRCLE

Opposite With Charlie, the ventriloquist doll, who played a major part in their stage shows over many years.

Right Charlie as he is today! Sporting a much tighter haircut, and thus keeping up with the times.

Below Another training session of the showbiz football team predictably descends into farce.

Overleaf Football press opportunities accompanied every season that a show was in town. Eric is standing in front of the post, Ernie fourth from left and Ken Dodd is far right.

not sharing that faith, and Eric and Ernie being prohibited from contributing to the writing and style of the show they were supposedly fronting, it is clear to see why it was destined for disaster.

It would be seven years before they had their own television series again but television was a very new medium, and that is why the theoretical setback that the boys should have suffered never really came to pass. In reality, it simply showed what we all understand today – that television has an immense power and influence over the public. This perceived, shattering failure, which is what it should have been, led to them appearing back on stage billed as "Those Stars of television – Morecambe and Wise". Television was proving what every veteran of a Blackpool summer season already knew – that you couldn't really do badly, as long as your name is out there for all to see. And Eric and Ernie were a well-honed, superb live act, and were soon back on course again.

But the pain would last, and as Ernie noted, "contrary to how the public saw him, (Eric) was a very insecure person at heart".

And the pain was shared – for Sadie and George proudly

The Palace/Savoy, Scunthorpe	The Grand, Croydon
The Theatre Royal, Lincoln	The Aston Hippodrome,
The Tivoli, Grimsby	Birmingham
Boscombe Hippodrome	The Richmond Theatre
Bristol Empire	The Empire, York
The Bedford, Camden Town	The Theatre Royal, Chatham
The Hippodrome, Norwich	The Hippodrome,
The Palace, Burnley	Wolverhampton
The Empire, Kilburn	The Grand, Southampton
The Palace, Grimsby	The New Theatre, Northampton

watching their charges in Morecambe it must have felt catastrophic. As my mother Joan explained, "The trouble was, Sadie and George lived in a small confined community. People could therefore be very cruel to them without realising it..."

Interesting to add to the north-south divide argument is my mother's further comment. "I watched *Running Wild*, and I didn't think it was that bad. And usually I was a very good judge of their comedy." So maybe the press did have it in for these "northern upstarts" appearing on the BBC, based in the south and transmitting from London.

Eric's ironic final line on the passing of the *Running Wild* era – and one that came to amuse him greatly when they would later get television viewing audiences of over 20 million – came in an interview shortly after the catastrophe, where he explained that they (Morecambe and Wise) would be okay "so long as we stay away from television...".

At the outset of their partnership, Eric and Ernie had been a team of two taking on the world. Morecambe and Wise were now both married – indeed, Eric had the start of a family, which I would join in April 1956. There was now less of a need to "take on the world" and far more of a desire to be with their own loved ones when away from the spotlight.

Their working relationship remained the same throughout their whole working life. This was chiefly due to the building blocks having been put in place from the earliest of ages, meeting up as 13-year-olds, sharing digs (even beds) and taking the bumpy road together to eventual glory. And the work continued. After the first summer season at Blackpool in '53, panto that winter took them to Sheffield with Stan Stennett topping the bill. A life-long friendship ensued, and it was with some irony that Eric's final performance, after which he would collapse and die in the wings of the theatre, was at the Roses Theatre, Tewkesbury, Stan's own theatre.

Summer season and winter panto would be the staple diet for Morecambe and Wise until Eric's heart attack in 1968, when the

decision to drop all such work and concentrate solely on their TV shows and Christmas specials would be taken.

During the panto season, theatre managements were not too keen on the idea of their artistes travelling too far over the Christmas break, fearful that a sudden change in weather conditions might prevent them getting back. It was usual, therefore, for the show's cast to end up sticking fairly close together and a camaraderie inevitably developed within each theatre's company. Ernie and Doreen would quite often throw a Christmas party for fellow cast members who couldn't risk heading for home during the festive break.

With the encouragement of Stan Stennett, a fellow devotee of the towable home, Eric had by now got into caravans, one of which was regularly attached to the rear of his Austin Hereford. Blackpool was particularly convenient, as they and any performing artistes were allowed to park their caravan at the Squires Gate Holiday Camp, which in fact was *not* a caravan site at all. My mother Joan had reservations. "Every time the wind got up, the sand would fly into the site and smother the windows and everything else."

The caravan period was initially fun, but with baby Gail now a toddler, and the author of this book close to making an appearance, the caravan had to go.

The Fifties ticked on very nicely, but with each successive year,

Left Eric and Ernie's popular appearances in Bruce Forsyth's Palladium show, which was massive in its day, really helped establish Morecambe and Wise as household names.

Above Right Billy Marsh (centre) talks to Norman Wisdom (seated left) and the director John "Paddy" Carstairs.

both Eric and Ernie began to feel a different kind of concern to one of money or employment, which had previously been all that they worried about. Now they were fretting about stagnation. Whether this triggered the very last time they would ever bring up the idea of going their separate ways is difficult to ascertain. It must surely have played a major part.

In an interview with a journalist in the Fifties, Eric commented, "If we don't make it really big soon, then the real success will never happen. We will forever coast along being very comfortable without becoming big stars."

In a dressing room after yet another reasonable performance on a reasonable show on a reasonable bill, Eric made it plain to Ernie that if things didn't get better for them, then he was calling time on the partnership. At that same moment – and if this were a Hollywood movie, you'd spill your popcorn at the unlikeliness of it – the stage doorman brought in a telegram. The message was an invitation to join Winifred Atwell on a six-month tour of Australia. That invitation altered entertainment history. Both Eric and Ernie, who had made several television appearances on *The Winifred Atwell Show* which had proved very popular, were thrilled at the opportunity of doing something fresh, and visiting a new continent in the process.

The big problem for Eric and Joan Morecambe was that they had two very young children. The problem-solver was Sadie and George, and we young children found ourselves transported north to Morecambe, a period about which I naturally have only a limited recollection.

Australia – three months in Sydney, three months in Melbourne – was a personal triumph for the boys, and one of the highlights of their working life. My mother still talks of the fun and laughter they all shared, the events they attended, the people they met, the warmth they were shown.

But while all that was well and good, the news from the British Isles was that variety was now dying a lot faster than had been anticipated. As Ernie said of this time, "The variety theatres everywhere had begun shutting their doors. But it was worse for us, because the Butterworth circuit of theatres – for which our agent Frank Pope had the sole booking – had closed down. This left him with virtually nothing to offer us."

In London, particularly, theatres were adapting just to survive. The Shepherd's Bush Empire became a television studio. The Coliseum, built in 1904 specifically for variety shows, is now the home of English National Opera. Many, like the Hackney Empire, became bingo halls, though some were eventually returned to something close to their former glory by becoming venues for the alternative, and then stand-up, comedy scene.

With television threatening the existence of Frederick Butterworth's variety halls, he did try to keep his theatre doors

Right Another of the wonderfully naïve publicity shots of the era, with their wives and Ernie "force-feeding" Eric oysters.

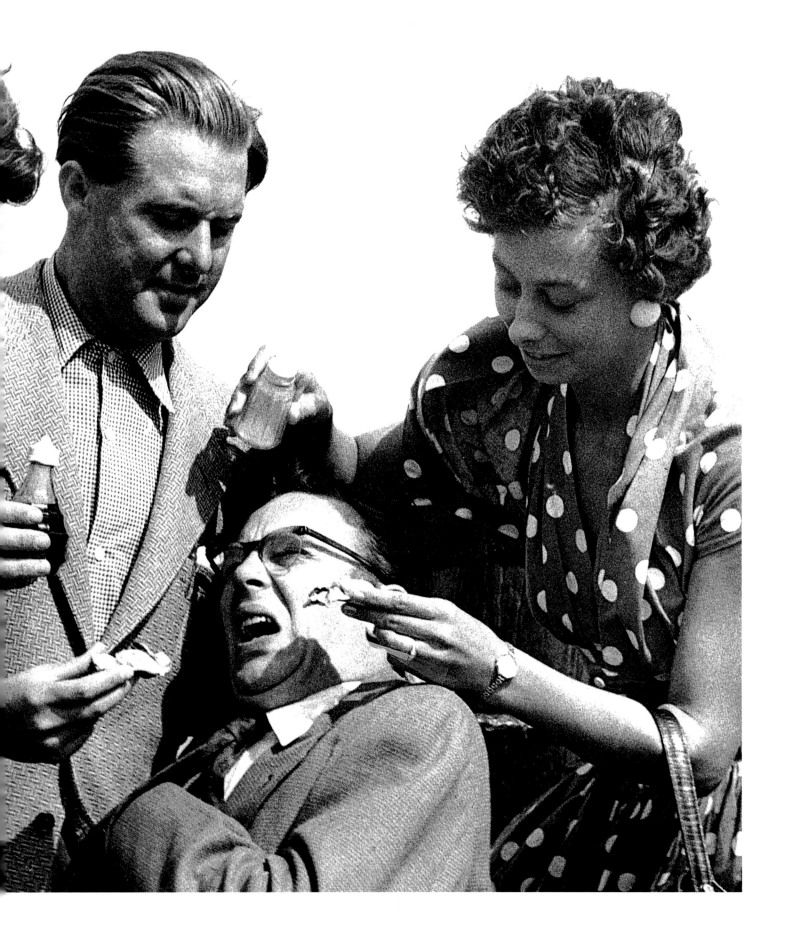

open. Sadly, the harsh economics of it all meant he was forced into having to dismiss many of his staff and then, arguably a little unwisely, took to promoting saucy reviews while banning mainstream press. For the likes of Frank Pope, and by direct association Morecambe and Wise, it meant the end of a particularly remarkable era in British entertainment. Ultimately, the very private Mister Butterworth, who had so shunned publicity that apparently no record exists of him having ever been interviewed, conceded defeat and dropped out of the variety entertainment business to concentrate almost solely on his holiday hotel interests. It's worth considering that when Eric and Ernie departed British soil for their Australian tour, Butterworth had under his name the list of theatres shown above. Very, very few remained in his hands by the end of the 1950s, and even fewer as places of variety entertainment.

On their return, therefore, Eric and Ernie were finding that, because of their six-month absence and because there were so few variety dates, they were having to make do with second- and third-rate bookings, the likes of which they were no longer accustomed to and no longer wanted to have to accept.

It was abundantly clear that, just to survive, they needed to scrutinise their situation and make a big decision. They had certainly made their mark as a talented and popular double act, so what was required next was both simple and plain obvious. They needed to break into television. Not like before. There would be no more second chances. This time they somehow had to approach it from a position of power – or *shared* power, at least. They were not so young and naïve, and carried a bit of a track record. But to succeed in their new goal of forging a career in the world of television, they needed a specialist agent. That meant contemplating the unenviable task of telling their friend and current agent – and my godfather – Frank Pope, that his services would no longer be required. As my mother puts it, "Sad though it was, it was make-or-break time in (Eric and Ernie's) careers, so there really was no room for sentiment."

Billy Marsh was already on his way to becoming a legend of the entertainment industry when Eric and Ernie came knocking at his door. Outside show business, Billy was a little like Frederick Butterworth, virtually unknown and happy for it to remain that way. He let the Grades and Delfonts, who dominated that era and alongside whom he formed part of the entertainment establishment, attract the fame and the attention. He may have preferred to remain in the wings, but Billy was always there and would one day employ a very young Michael Grade, as well as, some years later, me.

The greatest thing that happened for Eric and Ernie on their first encounter with Billy Marsh was discovering that he was already a fan of their act. Many, many years later, when I first began working in Billy's office (as replacement for Michael Grade, who went on to have a ludicrously successful career of his own), my father would reiterate that point to me. And the nicest thing

of all is that, at the end of almost every working day back in the mid-Seventies, Billy would summon me to his office, where he would pour himself and me a whisky before reminiscing about those early days and about Morecambe and Wise in general. So often he would wind up the conversation with, "I love your father. He's a genius! A genius!" I found it touching at the time, and still deeply touching now, but the really significant thing is that Billy really *understood* the boys from the very outset.

A meeting of these men could mean only one thing: success.

Without ever having a contract between them, Billy Marsh began getting them spots on television – indeed, he fixed two spots while chatting with them at their first meeting. The only thing Billy warned them about was material: "Television gobbles up material and once you've used it you can't use it again." Very unlike variety tours, in other words.

That meant a strategy needed to be created. Billy had to get the boys a series, and then writers who would work with them on material. Eric and Ernie recalled only too well what it was like having writers before, but Billy was shrewd and knew of two men – Dick Hills and Sid Green – who had written for Harry Secombe, Bruce Forsyth, Roy Castle and another popular double act of the Forties and Fifties, Jewel and Warriss. To produce the series, he wanted Colin Clews, someone whose work they, and most others in the business, greatly admired. Billy just had to convince Lew Grade, then head of ATV, that Grade wanted them.

When Billy first approached Lew Grade he seemed appreciative of the boys' talents, but wasn't so sure that they warranted a series. Perhaps he then got word back that Billy Marsh was looking to place his new charges on television elsewhere, for he soon came back to Billy having changed his mind.

The working relationship between Morecambe and Wise and Hills and Green would last seven years, and include not just the *Two of a Kind* ATV series (that would be the title of their show), but also three feature films they would make in the mid-Sixties for the Rank Organisation at Pinewood Studios, and the very first series they would do for the BBC when they left Grade in 1967.

Without doubt, it was a very successful pairing putting Morecambe and Wise with Hills and Green, but it wasn't always relaxed, particularly between Eric and Sid. In terms of working together, they never really argued badly, but both men were quite stubborn, and Eric had ideas that he felt he knew would work better for them. I, personally, tended to feel that Hills and Green honestly believed they deserved equal billing with the boys on the show, and that from there, perhaps, stems the disquiet that emerged between them.

When audience ratings for *Two of a Kind* went through the roof, vying in popularity with *Coronation Street*, and the show started earning them various awards, Hills and Green still saw it as their show as much as it was Eric and Ernie's. But, as Eric and Ernie saw it, *Two of a Kind*, *The Morecambe and Wise Show*, was precisely that. It wasn't *Four of a Kind*, *The Morecambe and*

Wise and Hills and Green Show. Everyone got on well enough, however, and the only occasionally ruffled feathers apparently belonged to Eric and Sid.

I met both Sid and Dick many times, and met Sid Green twice long after my father had gone, finding them both sincere, friendly and kind men. Sid had an air of negativity to Dick's positivity, but that was quite endearing. And I do think it must have been difficult for them to have found themselves contracted to write for a couple of lads from the variety circuit, who, by the second series, were two of the biggest names in television. For that is what happened in the 12 months separating 1961 and 1962.

The most important thing of all was that Morecambe and Wise now had a great agent who would stay with them for life, and a successful television series that would never go away – even outliving its stars. Yet the first series of *Two of a Kind* had nearly got off to the same sort of disastrous start that had befallen *Running Wild*.

Left Lew Grade, owner of Association TV and the man who gave Eric and Ernie their breakthrough television series of 1961, *Two Of A Kind*.

Below Sid Green and Dick Hills, the writers of Morecambe and Wise's *Two Of A Kind* series.

COVENTRY THEATRE
Hales Street Coventry
Telephone 23141

Administrator: J. M. Sykes   Manager & Licensee: G. K. Robinson

Fri, Sat, Sun, 26, 27 & 28 Feb.   Fri. at 7.30, Sat, Sun. at 6.00 & 8.30

Seats: Stalls £1.25 (25/-) £1.05 (21/-) 90p (18/-) Circle £1.25 (25/-) £1.05 (21/-) 90p (18/-)
Upper Circle 55p (11/-) Box Seats £1.25 (25/-)

Printed by Hastings Printing Company, Drury Lane, Hastings, Sussex. Telephone: Hastings 2283/4 & 2450

ITEM 1

"Television gobbles up material and once you've used it you can't use it again."

Billy Marsh

Opposite A poster advertising Morecambe & Wise's show "On the Stage!" at the Coventry Theatre in 1971. Their early 1970s tour was so successful for Morecambe and Wise that Eric came to nickname them the "bank raids"! Their agent Billy Marsh filmed the live show when it reached the Fairfield Halls, in Croydon in 1973.

HIPPODROME
BRISTOL

Chairman—PRINCE LITTLER   TELEPHONE — 21091   Manager—GEORGE A. HIGGS

MONDAY, NOV. 19

BERNARD DELFONT presents
THE FAMOUS "DECCA" RECORD & T.V STAR

6.25 TWICE NIGHTLY 8.40

★ **JOAN** ★
REGAN

SINGING HER TOP-SELLERS   AT THE PIANO: JOHNNY ROBERTS

★ # MORECAMBE AND WISE

"YOU'RE ONLY YOUNG ONCE"

★ # AUDREY JEANS ★

THE DECCA & TELEVISION COMEDY STAR

★ # JACK WATSON ★

B.B.C. DISC-JOCKEY ENTERTAINER

JACK ANYTHING GOES FRANCOIS	THE SKYLONS	REY & RONJY
	SENSATIONAL AERIALISTS	RON SCOTT

TRIBE BROS., LTD., London & St. Albans

Opposite Creeping up the bill, Eric and Ernie are second top at the Hippodrome in Bristol on this poster. While they were performing in the show, they heard a knock on their dressing-room door and were greeted by Bristol-born Cary Grant. Eric and Cary kept in contact down the years, meeting once a year for lunch in London when Grant was over from America on an annual visit to his mother.

Above A receipt from Eric and Ernie's agency, the National Theatrical Variety Agency. Frank Pope was Morecambe & Wise's agent throughout most of the 1950s, getting them on the Butterworth tour – a fine variety circuit second only to the Moss Empires' tour.

Stars
at
Last

The problem Morecambe and Wise had with their new series *Two of a Kind* for Lew Grade's ATV was a virtual replica of the fundamental problem they had encountered seven years earlier at the BBC with *Running Wild*. In the first script Hills and Green wrote for them, which screened in October 1961, they were lost in a large cast, back to being part of a crowd scene. The intimacy for which they had become well known through their variety theatre touring work was something everyone other than Eric and Ernie appeared to want them to leave behind.

Left Morecambe and Wise advance from TV stars to stars of the Big Screen. This still is from *The Intelligence Men* (1965), the first of their three films for the Rank Organisation, and shot mostly at Pinewood Studios.

Both men felt they were simply being overwhelmed by numbers, and a spoof spy sketch in that first show made Eric remark, "There were so many people in that sketch that I couldn't even find Ernie."

Eric and Ernie's concerns were not really given the attention which it would soon be proved that they merited. Fate then played a hand when Equity, the actors' union, decided at that precise moment to go on strike. The strike lasted exactly 12 weeks, which was supposed to be the recording schedule for the rest of the *Two of a Kind* series. Instead of being deemed a calamitous event, it proved to be the making of Morecambe and Wise and their television career.

At that time there were two unions for performers. As well as Equity, there was the Variety Artistes Federation, or VAF as it was affectionately called. The Equity strike was great from Eric and Ernie's perspective, as they were members of VAF, and weren't obliged to stop working. The majority of actors, however, were

aligned with Equity, so when it came down to recording the rest of the series, only Eric and Ernie, along with Hills and Green and virtually no one else, were able to film.

Suddenly Morecambe and Wise had a show that connected with their audience. More intimacy, tighter scripts. The cast of thousands would, fortunately, never return.

The boys would never look back as *Two of a Kind* became increasingly popular with the viewing public. By 1963, it was second only to *Coronation Street* in the top 20 television ratings, and Morecambe and Wise were voted Television Light Entertainment Personalities of the Year.

Michael Grade, a family friend and former Head at the BBC, ITV and Channel 4 (and many other job titles to boot) noted, "In the end, it was the intelligence of Eric and Ernie, the understanding of their craft, which enabled them to make the transition to television."

My mother, Joan, said, "In his work, Eric was a perfectionist. Once he and television had found each other, he was hooked."

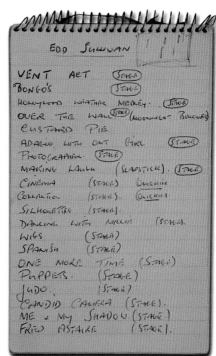

But being a star of television – maintaining the high standard and satisfying audience expectation – was the beginning of an inexorable rise in stress and tension for Eric. As his son, I know that he wasn't very good at switching off. He told me once that he dared not switch off in case he never could switch on again!

Ernie was made of different stuff. Ernie always struck me as a person who could view his work primarily as a job to be done, difficult in many ways, yet pleasant and privileged, too, but nonetheless a job. Ernie could end a day at the studios and leave all that their business entailed back there. Eric felt unable to do that. In fairness, Eric, as the one fated to become known as the comic genius, was always aware that he was carrying the show: everything, ultimately, came down to him. And that is not an arguable point. The show totally revolved around Eric. Eric was the funny man with extraordinary funny bones and, supremely brilliant as Ernie was – "irreplaceable" was how my father put it to me – he was always, as he once acknowledged fairly early on in their careers, always destined to be "…and Wise".

Above left Eric and Ernie disliked the Midnight Matinée performance. It was a late show put on for a specific charity or charities, but each act used it as a platform to outdo the other acts, and, in Eric's opinion, in a way that didn't suggest gentle messing around and easy banter.

Above centre Ernie's schedule for one of the Ed Sullivan shows. The vent act, the Bongos, Over the Wall and Me and My Shadow were big routines in their later touring years in the UK.

Above right One of the duo's many appearances the other side of the pond on *The Ed Sullivan Show*. Sullivan was a big star, and their appearances were designed to introduce the double act to a much bigger audience.

Opposite Eric and Ernie point to one another on television. By the mid 1960s Morecambe and Wise are undoubted stars of the small screen.

Ernie adjusted to and accepted that premise of their working relationship with good humour and immense dignity. After all, it became abundantly clear that it would invariably be Eric who would attract the full-on attention; be the one the press most often quoted; be the one expected to raise a laugh both socially and publicly. Perhaps this gave Ernie the opportunity to step back and be more pragmatic, more thoughtful about what Morecambe and Wise were doing. He could afford to be less intense on a 24/7 basis than Eric. One thing that can safely be assumed is that, had both men shared similar personalities, the partnership would never have been successful. It needed this combination of opposites, and it needed it in two men who had become friends in childhood, bringing a shared history to their work.

It should also be noted here that Ernie handled the business side of the partnership. Ever since Sadie had returned home to husband George, Ernie had been the one wheeling and dealing and fighting on the business front of their act. In ten years, they had gone from a first appearance on a Blackpool bill to being the top television comedians. The television shows would continue, but they would also be serenaded on two other fronts, the first lying across the Atlantic.

The television mogul, presenter, and former journalist Ed Sullivan was a regular visitor to Britain, with the sole purpose of scouting talent. He had already latched on to Norman Wisdom, taking the talented comic to the States to appear at his theatre. Next it was the turn of Morecambe and Wise, whom he first saw on Bruce Forsyth's show at the London Palladium in 1961. He was immediately impressed, and offered them $5,000 a show to make three appearances for him in New York.

The American public greeted them well, if not resoundingly so. It must have been a little strange for them facing luke-warm

Eric Morecambe
Ernie Wise

EXCLUSIVELY REPRESENTED BY:-
FRANK POPE NATIONAL THEATRICAL
VARIETY AGENCY LTD.

QUEENS HOUSE,
LEICESTER SQUARE,
LONDON, W.C.2.

TELEPHONES: GERRARD 4877-8-9
TELEGRAMS: NATVARY . LESQUARE . LONDON

Opening Eric dancing with girl who suddenly stands on is toe. Where he goes
kinto crazy movements. Waiter comes over to him and says a
gentlemen swould like to speak to. him.

Ernie. How do you do. Imre an agent and I represent Rock and Roll promotoi
I like that dance you just did its got something can you sing too.
Would you like to go on the stage be a big star.

Eric. Ill have to ask my Mother first.

Ernie. Your Mother you love your Mother thats good the kids will love that.

He loves his widowed Mother. To secreary.

Eric. What about me father.

Ernie. You havnt got a father have you. Oh the deals off.

Eric. Ill get rid of him he's only a little fellow Ill send him for a walk
on the M.1.

Ernie. Okay do it before Tuesday.

Eric. I cant he doesnt come out of prison untill Thursday

Ernie. Your Fathers in Prison.

Eric. Im afraid so

Ernie. Afraid so why thats perfect the kids will love it. Your a delinquent
whats he in for.

Eric. For something he didnt do.

Ernie. What didnt he do.

Eric. He didnt run fast enough.

Ernie. Okay get rid of your Mother . The contract (Big wad of paper) sign
here,

Eric. My Mother says I must not sign anything unless I read it first.

Ernie. But you just got rid of your Mother what does your father say.

Eric. He's in prison.

Ernie. Alright Im your Father look at me.Son I want to talk to you.

Eric. Yes Dad.

Ernie. I think you should sign this contract with this nice kind Gentlemen.

Eric. Alright Dad.

-64-

ERIC MORECAMBE and ERNIE WISE

Verse.

There is a man comes down our street
Once only every year
And when he comes he brings with him a sackfull of good cheer.
HE VISITS ALL THE CHILDREN IN OUR SINGLE NIGHT

He's a swinging father christmas with a sackfull of toys
Hes got a whole scene going for the little girls and boys
He wont come through the window he wont come through the door
he's a real way out santa who know's what the chimneys for
He will sneak into the bedroom and with a seasonal grin
Fill your christmas stocking right up to the very brim
Then off he LL go without delay. With his real hep riendeer
and his cool cool sliegh
He visits all the children in one single night

COUPLE ON THEIR HONEYMOON.
HOW DO YOU KNOW
HE'S GOT HIS PYJAMAS ON.

I HAVE A DUTY TO MY PUBLIC

YOU OWE NOTHING TO YOU PUBLIC FORGET HIS

WONDERFUL AUDIENCE

JUST LOOK AT THEM. I'LL BET THEY'L GO MAD

WHEN THEY WAKE AND FIND OUT

THEY ARE

OUR KIND OF AUDIENCE

THERE ALL DRUNK

LAST TANGO i PARIS

VICTOR SYLVESTER

JESS YATES. ORGANIST

Morecambe & Wise

Blackpool.

What do you want.

Im waiting for Daisey.

She's not here.

I suppose your waiting for Daisey.

No I am Daisey.

W. Thats a nice guitar. Its an Ivor Morance.

M. What ~~Ivnbvöxrbnmn~~...

W. Ivor Morance.

M. Ive got a Vauxhall. A friend of mine borroed it yesterday and he
was stopped by a policeman who said Whats your name, he said Weather-
all. the policeman said.. What makes this car.. he said Vauxhall..
The policeman said   Whats in the boot? mt friend said his foot....
(nothing)....

W. Thats Maureen Rose isnt it?

M. Yes, thats Maureen Rose.. she sat on my lap last night..

W. What happened?

M. Maureen Rose.

W. Vic Oliver is very sensitive about his hair.. which is odd really..
he doesnt have any...'.

M. (to band) and lets finish to gether this time.. I'm tired of wi
winning.......

M. Pull up a coffin and lie down...

M People have heard our music from one end of thee country to the other

W. Really?

M. Yes we play very loud.

M. And we would like you to know that we dont tell and blue or risque
jokes do we?

W. No

M. We tell no jokes that I wouldnt tell in front of my mother..and
h

"Eric was a huge generator of good energy. Everyone had to have a good time."

Francis Matthews

Previous pages and opposite Pages of scripts written by Ernie: as with Eric, Ernie kept many jottings and scripts. Putting this book together has revealed Ernie Wise to be far more creatively involved in their scripts and gags than originally thought.

-68-

Your Royal Highness (I heard Noel Gordons here.) My Lords Ladies and Gentlemen Head Waiter Chef Door man Chambermaids voices over .

Im deeply touched but not has deep ly touched has you have been coming to this dinner.

The Albany is a very nice hotel I wish I could afford to stay here Im staying Empire Road.

You may not know this but the Albany burnt down five years ago it was the first time they had served anything hot.

I asked the manager for a room. He said do you want a room with a bath or a shower. I said whats the difference. He said you stand up in the shower.

At the moment I am writing a play its all about my sex life. Its called Much ado about Nothing.

Im fifty three tommorrow. Im getting past it Im thinking of getting in a younger man and using jump leads.

Ive just finished a play its biblical takes part in Ireland its called Sodom and Begorra.

Thankyou for all those nice things you have said about us and thnks for inviting me to Birmingham home of Crossroads

I once gave an audition for crossroads they turned me down I was word perfect.

I musnt be unkind there are some very famous people have appeared on Crossroads Sir Henry Irving Sarah Bernahard.

Its the only programme where they make the tea between the commercial breaks.

I musnt forgett Pebble Mill. They asked me to appear on Pebble Mill but Id rather work for money.

I missed the Motor show here they say they had a marvellous Russian Car called the Moscavitch Carmargue bodywork by Parke Ward on a T.34 tank chassis Vannesa bought one. She still cant get a taxi in Golders Green.

I once went dancing with Vanneaa she's such a tall girl. I said Id like to make passionate love to you. She said if you do and I ever find out there will be trouble. Not only couldnt I see where I was going I couldnt hear the band.

Ive not been this nervous since I was trapped in a lift with Larry Grayson known as close encounters of the third kind.

Ive got many happy memeries of Bi rmingham all thos lovely theatres would you believe in 1939 I played the Hippodrome with Jack Hyltons band. Pantomime Sleeping beauty I used to carry on the princess the size of Janet Webb and say the princess has pricked her finger never got it wrong once.
The Alexander Sinbad the Sailor Dereck Salberg. Windsor Bearwood in variety Theatre Royal Wolverhampton Aston Hippodrome there was this old comic and they said when you die where would you like to be buried he said somewhere peacefull and quiet where no footsteps have ever been. In front of the box office of Dudley Hippodrome.

Of course Birmingham as changed quite alot now all that concrete it dehumanises everything.

All this mugging still I suppose it keeps the young people out of trouble. They tell me they have got a polite mugger he says one lump or two.

And the public toilets all that writing on the walls Meet me at six signed Frenchy its disgusting there never there.
I will leave you with this thought. three the average couple make love twice a week there are six billion people in this world and taking in to consideration children old age there are three hundred people have had a better time than you have since I started this speech . This is Ernie Wise News at ten Albany.

audiences by the mid-Sixties, as they were now such huge stars back in Britain. Anything less than open adoration must have seemed decidedly uninspiring, bringing back memories of the comparative tediousness of the Butterworth touring days.

But the visits to the States remained regular over a four-year period in the mid-1960s, recording Sullivan's show in New York at CBS-TV Studio 50, between West 53rd and West 54th in Manhattan, now appropriately known as the Ed Sullivan Theater. Ernie always enjoyed this American excursion. Working in the same country that had titillated his boyhood dreams of a Hollywood that even he most likely knew was a fantasy never failed to put a smile on his face and a spring in his step. In fact, doing the Sullivan shows with Eric as a partner must have been a bit of a downer.

His partner never really warmed to the whole idea, although Eric as often said, "the money was great!" which always amused me. A clear case of financial benefit over creative merit.

Opposite Eric "ruins" a xylophone performance by Ernie during a Stateside appearance on *The Ed Sullivan Show*. American audiences did not take to the duo's humour straightaway. Morecambe and Wise made 12 appearances on the show between 1963 and 1968.

Below The pair in director's chairs, on set at Pinewood Studios.

For Eric, the sidewalk was a pavement, the elevator a lift, the apartment a flat. The ultimate insult (as he saw it) was when the producer asked if he and Ernie could speak slower so the audience could understand what they were saying.

Eric would, however, not without a little nostalgia, talk fondly of those years with Sullivan, admitting that, were it not for his life-threatening illness lurking just around the corner, they would have carried on flying to and fro for as long as required.

Comedian, writer and massive Morecambe and Wise aficionado, Ben Elton, observed that it is possible that Eric's disenchantment with performing in the States had more to do with an inner conviction that he and Ernie could never have made it big over there however many times they had visited.

"I suppose it's possible," said Elton, "but I have to say that I think it's very unlikely. And I'm sure Eric must have known that."

It is true that Eric said he didn't want to spend the next 20 years of his life trying to make it in the States, having spent the same amount of time doing in back in Britain.

Elton remarked, "Far too many British entertainers break their hearts worrying about success in America. Look where it got Hancock. I think that Morecambe and Wise in the States would have become worse and worse and ended up as an impression of an American act, which would have been ludicrous."

PATRON

HER MAJESTY QUEEN ELIZABETH
THE QUEEN MOTHER

WE THE UNDERSIGNED
TENDER OUR SINCERE CONGRATULATIONS TO

Ernest Wise

ON BEING ONE OF THE REPRESENTATIVE ARTISTES
SELECTED TO APPEAR BEFORE

HER MAJESTY QUEEN ELIZABETH THE QUEEN MOTHER

ON THE OCCASION OF THE

ROYAL VARIETY PERFORMANCE

HELD AT THE

PRINCE OF WALES THEATRE
LONDON

on Monday, November 6th, 1961

THE PERFORMANCE BEING IN AID OF THE
VARIETY ARTISTES BENEVOLENT FUND AND INSTITUTION

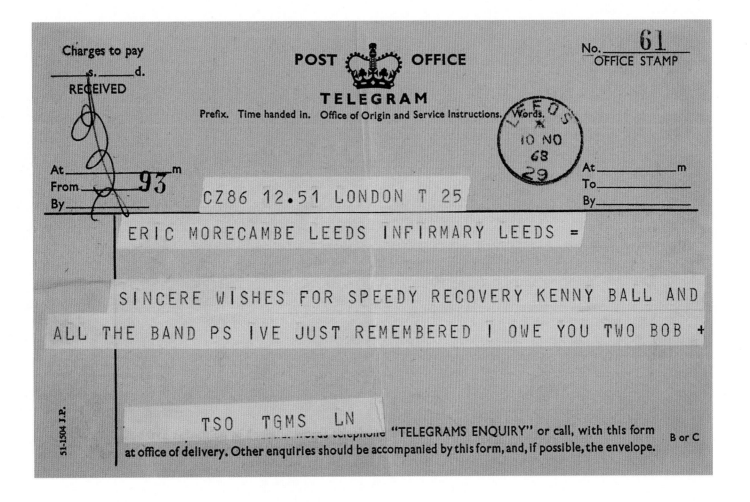

POST OFFICE

TELEGRAM

Charges to pay _____ s. _____ d.

RECEIVED

At _____ m

From _____ *93* m

By _____

Prefix. Time handed in. Office of Origin and Service Instructions. Words.

No. **61**
OFFICE STAMP

LEEDS
10 NO 68
29

At _____ m
To _____
By _____

CZ86 12.51 LONDON T 25

ERIC MORECAMBE LEEDS INFIRMARY LEEDS =

SINCERE WISHES FOR SPEEDY RECOVERY KENNY BALL AND

ALL THE BAND PS IVE JUST REMEMBERED I OWE YOU TWO BOB +

TSO   TGMS   LN

"TELEGRAMS ENQUIRY" or call, with this form at office of delivery. Other enquiries should be accompanied by this form, and, if possible, the envelope.

B or C

51-1504 J.P.

Above While recovering from his first heart attack in Leeds, Eric received many telegrams from well-wishers. This one is from Kenny Ball who, together with his Jazzmen, made many appearances on the Morecambe & Wise BBC shows.

Opposite The certificate received by Ernie for his appearance with Eric at the 1961 Royal Variety Performance. It bears the signature of Prince Charles in the bottom left-hand corner.

America became a pleasant distraction ended by illness, but it wasn't the only distraction. The boys were also about to star in movies. The order of the three films they would now set out to make for the Rank Organisation, based at Pinewood Studios was:

The Intelligence Men (1964)

That Riviera Touch (1966)

The Magnificent Two (1967)

All were produced by Hugh Stewart, and *The Intelligence Men* was directed by Robert Asher.

The British film industry boom was nearing its zenith by 1964. Built in 1935 by Charles Boot, and later sold to the Rank Organisation, Pinewood Studios lies 17 miles north-west of London. It was, and mostly still is, the home of the James Bond movies.

The studio was riding on a bit of a high when Eric and Ernie arrived to begin work in the autumn of 1964. The James Bond film *Goldfinger* had just been released, having mostly been filmed on the Pinewood stages and back-lots.

The actor Francis Matthews appeared in *The Intelligence Men* with Morecambe and Wise. Matthews was enjoying an enormous television career at the time of working with Eric and Ernie in series such as *Paul Temple*.

The Intelligence Men was a great job for Matthews to pick up. Not only was he on screen with the two biggest entertainers in television, but working with two other men who were his best mates – Bill Franklin and Terrance Alexander.

"We were all friends from the beginning," Matthews told me. "Bill, Terry, me, Eric and Ernie all gelled. I suppose it was because we were having such fun. Eric was a huge generator of good energy. Everyone had to have a good time."

Despite the pleasure taken from these projects and the fact that these three films have become cult classics (difficult to find a UK channel at the weekend on which one of them isn't being shown), it was an experimental foray into a genre where success, for the most part, would elude them.

Neither Eric nor Ernie regretted this cinematic interlude. Ernie would yearn to return to the big-screen more than Eric as the years

Top left Part of the poster campaign for Eric and Ernie's second film outing in *That Riviera Touch*, in 1966.

Above With their wives at Pinewood Studios for the signing of their film contract with Rank in 1964.

Below A mid 1960s publicity still for a Blackpool season. It took until the mid-1980s for this method of publicising panto and summer seasons to fall out of favour.

passed but they could afford to treat the movies as a sideshow because they knew they had a marvellous television career to slip back into. Television meant live audiences, and Eric and Ernie never worked better than when they had live audience response.

As the filmmaker and writer Bryan Forbes once told me, "If you've always worked in front of live audiences, the sudden shock of doing comedy on a silent stage, where all you can rely on is your director, is a major leap."

Comedian, family friend and former Goon, the late Sir Harry Secombe, believed that Eric and Ernie's three film outings did them few favours. "I don't think people knew how to handle them in this medium," he pointed out when interviewed in 1994. "Theirs was a raw talent in some respects, and sometimes that's too big for the screen. But Eric was capable of underplaying if directed properly and though these films weren't great, they weren't bad, either."

Personally, I have never been convinced that employing their television scriptwriters, Hills and Green, to do the screenplays for these films was the correct move. Certainly there was an obvious continuity in keeping a team together, but it might have been smarter, with the benefit of hindsight, to have kept the television writers as television writers, and pulled in film writers.

The films, however, were by no means a washout. As well as regular screenings on television today, I often come across people whom you would expect to enthuse about the Morecambe and Wise Christmas specials, but instead tell me how wonderful their films are. This is usually followed by, "especially *That Riviera Touch*". It is curious how that middle film has become a minor classic. The best thing with this middle film for Eric, Ernie, and their respective wives Joan and Doreen was that it was filmed mostly on location in the South of France. My mother still rates that time as perhaps the best of her life spent with Eric.

Top right With Francis Matthews and Anita Tibbles on the set of their BBC show in 1974.

Right Lionel Jeffries (far left), Tony Curtis and Suzanne Lloyd in the South of France during shooting of *That Riviera Touch*.

Actress Suzanne Lloyd guest-starred in that film. She told me that she sensed filmmaking took Eric and Ernie out of their comfort zone. "They were improv specialists. They did it once on television and that was that. In film they had to do it over and over, and matching was a nightmare for both of them.

"Eric was not always 'on,'" she said. "This was hard for them. I cannot stress this enough. They had a lot riding on this film, and they knew they were not in their element. But that doesn't mean there weren't laughs. There were a lot. The crew had a devil of a time not ruining a take by laughing out loud...."

Their final outing was *The Magnificent Two* (1967). Out of the three, this one always sits the most uncomfortably with me. It's based on the oldest of comic premises, mistaken identity. Yet, simultaneously, it has an undercurrent of violence – moderately cartoon in execution, but probably not enough so – running right through its core. When the actors are not playing it for laughs, their characters are just plain nasty. People get mown down with

guns in this film! Certainly, it is a long stretch from Eric and Ernie's television personas, while in other ways not being a long enough stretch from them. As with the two preceding outings, however, there are some fine comedic moments, particularly when it is just Eric and Ernie on screen.

The boys' flirtation with films came and went, and would much later make a brief swansong, but meanwhile it was back to what they did best. There were more television shows to make.

Above An off-camera still of Eric and Ernie with fellow cast members in the Black Woods near Pinewood Studios for a battle scene in the duo's final film for Rank, *The Magnificent Two*.

Opposite After success in television with their *Two Of A Kind* series for Lew Grade, Eric and Ernie received various advertising offers. This one for men's knitwear!

Overleaf The poster used to publicise Eric and Ernie's 1965 film *The Intelligence Men*.

The Rank Organisation presents

ERIC MORECAM

THEIR FIRST-AND FABULOUSLY FUNNY FILM

in Colour

as THE INTELL

WILLIAM FRANKLYN · APRIL OLRICH · GLO

Screenplay by S. C. GREEN and R. M. HILLS · Story by PETER

JGH STEWART Production

ERNIE
BE AND WISE

...GENCE MEN

PAUL · RICHARD VERNON · JACQUELINE JONES

...KMORE · Produced by HUGH STEWART · Directed by ROBERT ASHER

CHAPTER 7

The Dream Team

It was at Jimmy Corrigan's club in Batley, West Yorkshire, 7 November 1968 that it all imploded for Morecambe and Wise. Looking back all these years hence, recalling the treadmill they were on – the lack of stress-free time away from the television and film studios; flying to and from work in America; Eric's lively personality and need to be constantly switched on; the chain-smoking with no fresh air or exercise amid this almost nocturnal lifestyle – it is ludicrously clear that, even at the very young age of 42, Eric being struck down with a heart attack that so very nearly killed him was quite predictable.

As my mother puts its, "Eric lived on his nerves, always did. And he was always concerned about people's expectations. He never wanted to let the public or studios down. And at the back of his mind was that nagging thought that their career could end tomorrow, so it became natural to accept anything going; anything that was offered them."

Ernie said, "He wore himself out," something with which I completely agree. Living with him, one couldn't help but sense he had this inability just to ease up for a while, if only for the sake of his health. "When he was on stage, he was very dedicated," continued Ernie. "I don't have the same temperament as his, and I've always held something back." I find Ernie's observation of himself and Eric, both frank and touching. Maybe to become the comic genius people now recognise Eric to be, he had to be that driven, that motivated – not able to shut off for even a moment;

not able to keep anything back in reserve. It's back to that thing of not being able to start up again should he have risked shutting down for a short while.

Recovery was slow, because Eric decided that the stress of doing television meant he needed to take a longer break away from it than if he were returning to any other job. This made good sense, as he would never take so much time away from the partnership again, at least not until he had to undergo heart surgery some years later.

During the six-month sabbatical, my father reconnected with things that mattered and that, by his own admission, he had come to ignore. It was wonderful to go on very slow walks with

him beyond the golf course where his house still stands, and see him looking at the clouds, or taking out a pair of binoculars and doing a bit of bird watching. It's important to stress that during the first two months of his six-month recovery period, he literally did nothing. It was only after about three months that he had the sudden urge to get out into the wider world, and that was how we came to find ourselves in the stands at Luton Town Football Club; Watford playing away that particular weekend making the choice an easy one.

It was on the second or third visit to the ground that word got back to the Chairman of the club that this famous comedian was turning up to home games with his son. Within that first season of our going to the home games at Kenilworth Road, Luton, we were suddenly in the Directors' box, and by the second season, my father was on the board! Luton would remain his greatest passion away from showbusiness to his dying day, and my second to last outing with my father was at that very stadium only six months before his death in 1984.

Ironically, the heart attack brought about the situation the Morecambes and the Wises had all been so worried about and which had kept them working so hard – a sudden end to their careers and earnings.

In terms of their future, the *family's* future, I never sensed from being around my parents it was quite as bad as that. It became clearer within about three months that, first, Eric would be able to resume his partnership with Ernie and, second, not only would the BBC and the viewing public welcome them back, but Bill Cotton (then Head of Light Entertainment at the BBC) would reorganise their schedule around Eric's health. This would mean more rehearsal time, the end of the rushed, haphazard 30-minute

shows recorded as live, and in their stead the more thoughtfully rehearsed, 45-minute pre-recorded shows.

The great thing about this new format was that it would in due course, and with a major creative development, present them with the opportunity to nurture such ideas as the flat and bed routines.

From now on, everything was geared around Eric's health, and this would make a very big difference to his quality of life, which up until then had been sacrificed in the chase for fame and fortune. This state of being driven at all costs, this fear, particularly Eric's fear it should be noted, came from his absolute certainty that the Morecambe and Wise act would not last; that

Above left Eric recovers from his first heart attack in Leeds Royal Infirmary, November 1968.

Above right Props were a large part of *The Morecambe and Wise Show*. This "horse", from a Dick Turpin sketch in 1976, is one of my favourites.

Right Bill Cotton, Head of Light Entertainment at the BBC from 1970 until 1977.

Top left Eric and Ernie play mandolins during a Robin Hood sketch from 1971.

Top right In this sketch from 1976, the duo have their afternoon's sunbathing interrupted by some badminton-playing nudists from next door.

Above He's the man! Eric and Ernie pay due respect to their long-time BBC script writer Eddie Braben. It was Braben's idea to have the duo, not only living together, but sharing a double bed.

Left "Who are you calling slow-coach?" In this July 1969 sketch, Eric (and a long-haired Ernie) play tortoises emerging from winter hibernation.

FILM STILLS OF

THE INTELLIGENE
MEN !

1964   PINEWOOD
STUDIOS
RANKS
ENG

PLEASE TURN BACK.

Left and overleaf This extract of pages from a photo album in Eric's archives shows a collection of stills from the film *The Intelligence Men*, which Eric and Ernie starred in in 1965. Note the comments written by Eric on some of the pages towards the end.

SYD - DICK - ERNIE - IN CAFE.

TUTTE LEMCLOW

IN M.I.5. OFFICE.

THE GOODLOOKIN ONE

MADE IT! JAC JONES.

Opposite You know you've hit the big time when you get your own comic strip. Eric sports another variant style of wearing spectacles!

Opposite and overleaf An extract from one of Eric's notebooks from the early 1970s: wherever Eric could write notes or gags, he did.

Left In costume again, this time with the wonderful June Whitfield in a tea plantation sketch from November 1974.

Below "Look at me when I'm talking to you." Eric and Ernie relaxing backstage in their dressing room.

they had a shelf life; that suddenly no one would like them; that they would be yesterday's news and some mystic voice, as my father put it, would ask for it all back!

One thing that would not be the same again for Morecambe and Wise was who was writing the scripts. During Eric's convalescence, Hills and Green had moved on never to return. Ernie and his wife Doreen only discovered this fact on a flight from New York from a member of the crew, which was a little embarrassing. Eric took it very badly, "In fact, I was surprised how hurt he was," said my mother, Joan.

It wasn't the fact they had decided to call it a day with Eric and Ernie that upset the boys, but that they had absconded without a direct word to either of them after all those successful years working together.

It later transpired that the agent for Hills and Green had made it clear to Bill Cotton that they would carry on writing for Morecambe and Wise only if they were credited as executive producers on the show. That would never have happened back then at the BBC, so Hills and Green had a Plan B – an offer to do their *own* show for ATV had been made to them, and now they took it. They were never again to enjoy the same level of success that they had seen when writing for Eric and Ernie.

"In any event, I think their relationship with Hills and Green would have fractured anyway," said Michael Grade, "because I don't think Hills and Green ever gave Eric and Ernie full credit for what they achieved with their material."

Talented Liverpudlian writer, Eddie Braben, was summoned by Bill Cotton. He had written for Ken Dodd and many others, and was creating quite a name for himself.

"When Bill asked me to write for Morecambe and Wise, I said, 'No', " recalled Braben. "He asked me why not. And I replied, 'Because to be honest I don't think I'm good enough.' He said, 'Well, I think you are.'"

FILL LINES

AFTER SPECULATION.
"YOUR ON THE RIGHT LINE BUT
YOU'RE ON THE WRONG TRAIN"

WOMAN TALKING ABOUT MARRIED TO
SEX ??
"ARE YOU SLEEPING WITH ANY-
ONE LIKE"
"ONLY IN LOOKS"!

BECAUSE THEY LIKE AN INDIAN WASHING
MACHINE - A ROCK - ROCK.

RADIO DIALOGUE. (WHAT ARE YOU DOING

ROCK HERE - I THOUGHT YOU
LOVED HIM, THAT'S WHY YOU LEFT
ME -
I DID - BUT HE SUE LEFT HIM
WHY?
HE WAS TOO NICE)

ORANGE RINGS. WHO CAN THAT BE
I HAVE NO FRIENDS.

STRAIGHT: ITS YOUR HUSBAND.

YOU SEE I TOLD YOU I HAVE NO
FRIENDS.

SAW THAT SO MANY BOY FRIENDS -
WHY NOT, SHE ADVERTISES AT FOOTBALL MATCHES.

Q.) WHY IS THERE'S ONLY ONE LIGHT ON?
B. WHEN THE MUSIC IS BEETHOVEN.   THIS RECORD
NOT ONLY IS
HIS DEAF BUT HIS EYES WENT TO GOOD
HELD BAD TOO.

G. I WAS WAITING FOR FIDDLE BETTER.
B. I PRAYED FOR RAIN SO IT WOULD REFRAIN

ONLY
OCCASIONALLY FORGET A FACE -
BUT ITS YOURS.
THIS TIME.

SHE 'I'VE GOT SHARP EYES.
A. 'YOU GOT GREAT TITS TOO' X

DAD WILL GIVE YOU A LOCK OF MY HAIR
GIRL WILL GIVE YOU ONE OF MY HAIRS
BUT ONLY ONE?
APPLAUSE
BUT ITS ONE I CAN ILL-AFFORD -

HEY SPAGETTI FACE

FANNY SEEING YOU AFTER ALL
THESE YEARS - I THOUGHT YOU
WERE DEAD - YOU'RE NOT
ARE YOU?

SHOW I KIDDLED HER ON
THE ROOF.

VISUAL PICTURE GAG.
ZEBRA CROSSING WHERE CHURCH R.C.
LOLLIPOP LADY WITH LOLLY POP
WRITTEN 'STOP NUNS CROSSING NUNS
CROSS

LISTEN, WASN'T THAT A CAR?
IF IT ISN'T THERE'S SOMETHING WRONG
WITH THE HORSES LEGS   STELLA.

ARE YOU GOING TO APPLAUD
I DON'T LIKE?
THANK YOU VERY KIND

G. I NEVER EVEN KISSED A BOY UNTIL
I GOT MY DEGREE - (SEXY GIRL).
YOU MEAN YOU GOT A DEGREE FOR KISSING?

LIKE LUCERNE. I'VE SEEN YOU
WITH THAT.
POISON
LECTURE FORM.

(FEED BOX) NOBODY 'A BOTTLE A DAY
AND DON'T CALL WITH
FRIGHT

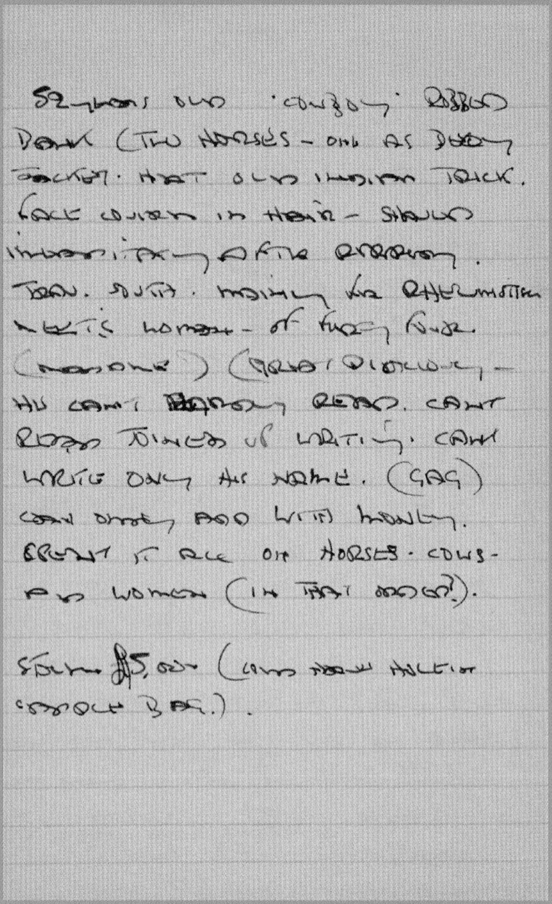

52 years old 'cowboy' robbed
bank (two horses - one as decoy
jockey. that old Indian trick.
fake cowboy in their - should
 immortality after bearation.
town. posse. making for Rattlemotten
meets woman - of their own.
(romance) (great dialogue,-
he can't barely read. can't
read joined up writing. can't
write only his name. (gag)
can only add with money.
spent it all on horses - cows -
and women (in that order?).

stole $5,000 (and saw half in
console box.)

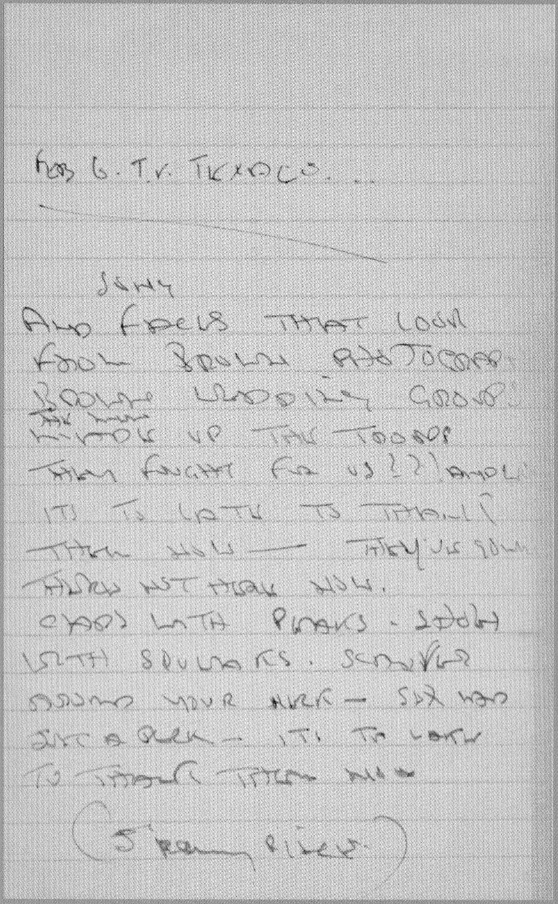

has G. TV. Texaco ...

                    Sony
and focus that look
fool. bloody photographer.
bloody wedding goons.
hands up the troops
they fought for us?? and is
it's to late to thank?
then how — they've gone
thanks not then now.
chaps with flowers - stood
with swords. scatter
round your area — say who
saw a deer — its to late
to thank them all

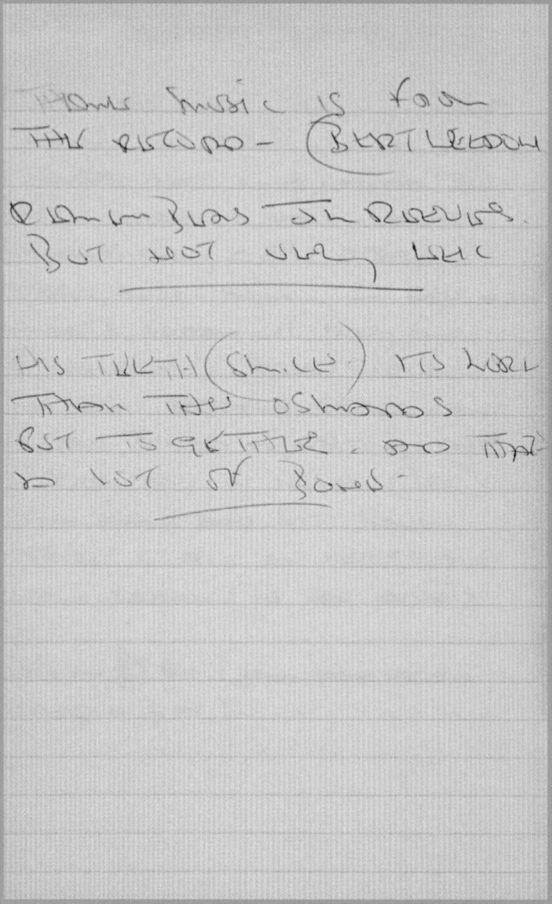

              (Sidney Riley.)

Theme music is for
that record - (Bert Weedon

playing bass in records.
but not very well

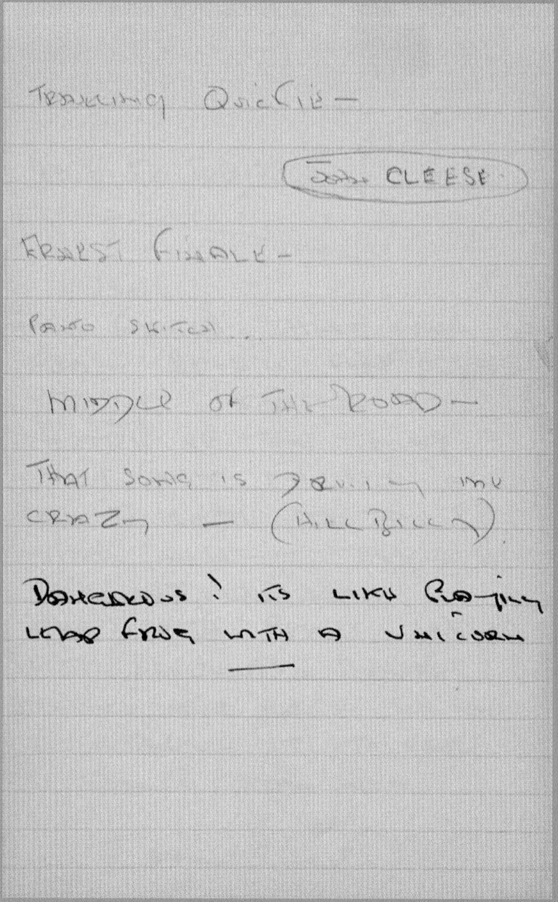

his teeth (smile) its worse
than the Osmonds
but is gentler. and that
is not TV bond-

Traveling Quickie —

              (John Cleese)

French finale —

piano sketch ...

middle of the road —

that song is driving me
crazy — (hillbilly)

dangerous! its like playing
leap frog with a unicorn

From Eric and Ernie's perspective, there was a mixture of excitement and anticipation, matched with genuine concern over the idea of Eddie Braben coming on board. I know that my father loved what Eddie had done for Ken Dodd, but pointed out that Morecambe and Wise were less about one-liners and more about sketches and situations, something they had been slowly developing over the last seven years with Hills and Green.

When they met up with Eddie and Bill Cotton at the BBC, it was evident within minutes that there was chemistry within the group. Instead of Eddie Braben being the wrong replacement for Hills and Green, it was clear that in fact he was the missing link – the connection between Morecambe and Wise and their viewing public. And one really has to wonder who, without Eddie as the third member of the double act (as he has rightly become known), would have driven them on to such great heights? With Hills and Green, they would surely have continued to create very good, entertaining shows. But it was the development of their on-stage personalities through the material that Eddie brought to the table that added a whole new dimension to Morecambe and Wise.

Mind you, I'm making it sound as if this was the immediate outcome of their first meeting. It wasn't. Indeed, they went their separate ways with Eric and Ernie still a little uncertain. Eddie had made it clear at the meeting that he would not be writing like Hills and Green. He would be sending them sample material for a new Morecambe and Wise, based on how *he* saw them.

Eddie Braben delivered his script, and Morecambe and Wise sat down to begin working on it along with John Ammonds. John had produced Eric and Ernie on the radio in the late Forties and Fifties and would remain with them for several years to come, working with them again at the very end of Eric's life. The only precautionary measure they took was to add a sketch by Mike Craig and Lawrie Kinsley. Craig would write again for Morecambe and Wise near the end of their career, and shared a good friendship with the boys. The show transmitted on 27 July 1969. It got a great response, and Braben was now as much a part of the partnership as Eric or Ernie.

Braben always believes he never interfered with Eric's character at all, but it was abundantly clear that Eric was no longer the snivelling idiot funny man of the variety halls that had drifted successfully into television. Eric was now a confident performer, sharing his mischief and mayhem with the viewing public via looks to camera and a relentless sending-up of his partner Ernie – slaps around the

Top left Eric, a onetime president of the Lord's Taverners, signs cricket bats for a charity auction with Prime Minister Edward Heath.

Top right This pipe was one of Eric's favourites, and is designed as a bird's head. The stem of the pipe forms the beak.

Above Actor Frank Finlay as Casanova in February 1973, with Ernie taking the dressing up a little further than usual, and Eric seemingly enjoying the fact!

refund. I and her spend over my limit. If you like a keys to see. I feel all disturbed and when I offered to pay with traveller cheques. they were treated with suspicion. Like the other I found old Clark they said he has no problems

Whilst you in a supermarket in Florida I just to pay for groceries with a 100 dollar bill length the 100 dollar note she examined stopped the name and velocity by the name. No you can accepted. So Cash credit card pin. No Cash credit card travellers cheques treated him with suspicion

My wife has just had plastic surgery. We cut up all her credit cards. Today the bank are dealing with the advantages of credit cards and travellers cheques. Of course all they are doing is playing on our sense of fear of being mugged. Myself being Yorkshire I'm very Suspicion of credit its plus is known has being betold to some one else play by Hard Cash Say it all its

All her came and queued up to show to interested Sheila even then he cannot afford it.

If had as they stole my wife credit card I should report it to the police. The thief has Sheila been there her. By the very loud you loan find no cash for the article.

then listed and a promise the real thief sped accepted with delight no suspicion.

It's a frightening thought that a piece of plastic is more important than the human smile or the hard stare. the fear had Sheila they cant the figure ten days. I have a card free of course I refuse to pay for one and I refuse to allow it is no way full of allow is. I save to loan to loan interest. I save to loan with credit plus I go away for a few years the day after I leave the credit card amount I leave the credit and never gets owing to four and never gets owing to four and building up to a hard and building up to a hard sum. They are not always worth can be refund. I just they pay a car rental you to pay a car rental you after my card and it pay

Cecil Wilson

MORECAMBE AND Me by Ernie
          WISE
(with a running commentary by Eric Morecambe)

(NOTE: This is as far as I can take the story
after one interview session with Ernie Wise. It
cannot be more than a draft until Eric Morecambe
is well enough to fill it out with his own memories
of the partnership and turn the whole operation into
a printed version of a double act,but I hope that
Ernie Wise's side of the story will give some idea
of the general framework.)

Opposite *The Morecambe & Wise Show* was entered for the Golden Rose of Montreux Award in 1970 and this is a speech that Ernie wrote while staying in Montreux for the Awards.

Above and overleaf An extract of pages from a transcript in Ernie's archives suggesting that he sat down with a ghost-writer and talked about his life before, and with, Eric for a book. Presumably, this later formed his autobiography *Still On My Way To Hollywood*.

2

For a while we were still billed as Master Ernest
Wiseman and Master John Eric Bartholomew. Eventually
Jack Hylton advised me to try a shorter name and I became
Ernie Wise. And Adelaide Hall's husband, Bert Hicks, said
to young Bartholomew: 'Why don't you change your name and
call yourself after the town you come from, you know, like
Jack Benny's Rochester' So as the boy came from Morecambe
he called himself Eric Morecambe. Now you know us as
Morecambe and Wise.

What made us chum up so well from the word go was that
we both came from the same kind of background. My father was
a railway porter in Yorkshire; Eric's was a corporation
labourer in Lancashire.

I had broken into the business as a kid by performing
as an amateur around the local clubs and pubs with my father.
Eric had done the same sort of thing as a solo comedy act in
Morecambe and also had quite a success in local talent contests.

I was born in a small terrace house in Wardour Street,
Leeds, and spent my childhood moving about Yorkshire wherever
my father's railway work took him.

We were a pretty poor family. I was the eldest of
five children -- one of them, Arthur, died at the age of five
from appendicitis, which could be quite a serious thing in
those days -- and my father had to bring us all up on about
£2 a week. So anything he could pick up on the side as an
amateur, or semi-pro, performer was more than welcome.

mf

3

He was a song and dance man. It was the habit
with his kind of working man's club act to model yourself
on a current star and Dad did an Al Jolson act. I joined
him at the age of six as a tap dancer. We would do a
Sunday night show at one of these clubs for 30s between
us. It was all highly illegal in my case and hardly
the sort of thing to send me to school the next morning
very fresh and eager to learn.

The education authorities soon put a stop to my
part of the act but we were so naive that we thought that
all we had to do to get round the law was to shift our
pitch. So we emigrated, as you might say, from Leeds to
Bradford.

We used to do a week-end package deal -- Saturday
night, Sunday dinner time and evening, all for £3.10s.
But only if we were lucky. It wasn't always as much as
that. The big thing was to be invited to join the club
members for dinner. 'Pie and peas', we called it.

I kept up that routine without getting caught again
by the school people until I was 12. Then I gave an
audition at the Leeds Empire for Bryan Michie. Again it
looked like a case of 'Don't call us; we'll call you' and
I heard no more for a long time. Then, just as I was
losing hope, I had a telegram from him inviting me to
London. He had mentioned me to Hylton and Hylton, with
his shrewd business brain, seized on me as a good
publicity gimmick.

4

He was doing a show called <u>Bandwaggon</u> with his
'boys', as he called his orchestra, at the Prince's
Theatre, now known as the Shaftesbury, and it just
happened that he badly needed a boost for his business.
So he took me on as a new comedy find and had me publicised
in a big way as a railway porter's son.

He paid me £6 a week. For that I walked on in a
sort of Chaplin outfit, with a little moustache, and sang
<u>I'm Knee Deep in Daisies</u>. I also did a bit of clog
dancing and told some corny gags. I still remember one
with a shudder. Two men standing on the street corner.
One says, 'What shall we do today? Let's toss a coin.
If it comes down heads we'll go to the pictures. If it
comes down tails we'll go to the football match. And if
it stands on end we'll go to work'. Terrible, I know,
but I was only 12.

For me that first taste of professional show
business was like a fairy story and Jack Hylton was like
a fairy godfather. There was not only the thrill of
meeting showmen like him and stars like Arthur Askey, but
the luxury of living in slap-up digs, first at the
Shaftesbury Hotel, near the theatre, and then at the top
of the old Fifty Restaurant in St. Martin's Lane. After
the plain meals I had been used to at home those hotel and
restaurant meals were something unbelievable.

Jack Hylton paid for all that. He took me under his
wing right from the start in the nicest fatherly way. He
seemed to re-live his own boyhood in me. He, too, had begun
as a lad by performing around the clubs and pubs and I
brought it all back to him.

mf

I remember going into his office one day and seeing him
sitting there with a great heap of money on the desk. It must
have been about £300. He casually picked out a ten shilling
note and said, 'Here you are'. It was the first ten shilling
note I had ever been given.

He also fitted me out with a complete wardrobe from
top to toe and when he thought my overcoat looked too thin for
the cold weather he bought me a new thick one.

He lived like a king with a luxury flat in Cumberland
Mansions, a house at Angmering on Sea and a chauffeur driven
Buick. But he never lost his simple north country touch and
having northerners like me in his show emphasised it all the
more. He had a meat pie sent to London every week from Bolton,
his old home town, and he would often call to me, 'Come on, Ern',
as he went into his dressing room between performances, to share
a plate of tripe with him. Cold tripe, I mean, the way we
always used to eat it in the north.

He even brought my father down to stay with me and
offered him a job to keep him in London, but Dad had been too
long on the railways by then to fancy a change of career and
when he went back to Leeds I was given a matron to look after
me as well as Maureen Potter, Maureen Flanagan and the other
kids in the show.

Mr. Hylton, as I always called him even after I'd grown
up, opened my first bank account for me. With all my living
expenses paid for I had my whole £6 a week to myself. I kept
£3 and sent the other three home. And they really needed it,
believe me. Years of working on the railway in all weathers
as a porter and lamp lighter were beginning to tell on my father.
His rheumatism turned to rheumatoid arthritis and he became so
ill and crippled with it that he was a permanent invalid from the
age of about 40.

mf

I toured with Jack Hylton's last show before the war.
Jack's Back he called it and the bills showed a familiar back
view of the plump, curly haired little man conducting his band.
I was 12½ then and went to a different school every week.
Sometimes I would run out for the lunch break to find the
Hylton Buick waiting with a chauffeur at the wheel to drive
me to a rehearsal.

When the war broke out he evacuated me to his house
at Angmering. The place was full of show people, George
Black, in those days the big boss at the London Palladium, had
a house there and the Crazy Gang all lived round about. I
moved into the Hylton household as one of the family with
his Austrian friend Fifi and his two young daughters, Georgie
and Jackie.

By that time Jack's band had dispersed and the London
theatres had closed down for what everyone expected to be the
obliteration of London. Fearing they would never open again,
I went back to my family. They were then living rather poorly
in Oxley Street, Leeds and my father said, 'Well, what have
you come home for?'

I had a friend up there who ran a coal round and to
tide me over for a while I helped him with his deliveries for
a few bob a week. Then when things got going again in the
theatre and it seemed that the blitz wasn't going to happen
after all, I joined Bryan Michie's Youth Takes A Bow. By
this time I was earning a fabulous £7 a week.

mf

7

That was when I met Eric Morecambe again. He was
doing a one-man Flanagan and Allan act; I was doing a sort
of Mickey Rooney. Eric was an only son. His father had
been badly hurt in a football match and was off work a lot;
his mother, who had always had a hankering after show business
herself and was smitten with the glamour of the stage,
travelled round the country with him. That was quite a
northern custom and the managements used to pay the
mothers' fares.

Eric's mother became almost as much a mother to me as
she was to him and one night in Oxford when I could find no
digs of my own she took me into theirs and let me sleep on
the li-lo in the front room.

In the show we had double acts like Moon and Bentley
(George Moon and Dick Bentley, who was still to make his name
in the Take it from Here radio team with Jimmy Edwards and
Joy Nichols). Eric and I used to study their style -- and
their material -- hoping to branch out in a double act of our
own. We also gorged ourselves on Laurel and Hardy and Abbott
and Costello films and worked out a routine from bits borrowed
from these and pretty well every other double act we had ever
seen.

We begged Jack Hylton to try us out together but we
could never get him interested, still, we kept on and on at
him until he let us have a go in a Youth Takes a Bow one
Friday night in 1940.

mf

8

After that it became a more or less regular thing,
I say 'more or less' because there was always a battle to
get the act in. If the show was running short of time our
poor old duo, billed by now as John Bartholomew and Ernie
Wise, was always the first to go.

Friends used to say, 'Why do you want to do a
double act? Supposing one of you is ill, what happens
to the other one?"

We always laughed that off and said we'd go on
together, come what may, but it wasn't so funny 28 years
later when Eric was off with a heart attack. It was the
first break in our act in all that time.

After Youth Takes a Bow we pressed on with this
double-act idea. We would grab every chance to work
together -- even an amateur show so long as there was a
pound in it. But we couldn't get on the Moss Empires
circuit and until we did that we were nowhere. Moss Empires
were the accolade of the variety profession: the real road
to the top.

Then, in 1941, came a real break. George Black,
then the chief of that circuit, gave us an audition for
Strike a New Note, the Sid Field show at the Prince of Wales
Theatre.

Black took us on because I think he admired the
nerve of us, especially in the bit where Eric walked across
the stage all nancified and the patter went like this:

Me: What are you walking like that for?

Eric: I'm a business man.

Me: A business man? But a business man doesn't walk like
                  that

Eric: Ah! But you don't know my business.

We had no idea what it meant. After all, we were barely 15.

mf

face; wig gags; short, fat, hairy legs gags; a blur of wit and gentle put-downs – a clear combo of Phil Silvers and Groucho Marx, with a nod or two in the direction of Jack Benny. The twisting of his glasses to the side of his head, for example, was a classic Benny visual gag and the idea of Ernie being parsimonious was also Benny's style.

"Eric gradually changed into a harder figure," is how my mother put it. "He was a kind of straight man who was funny as opposed to Ernie, who became the comic who tried to be funny but wasn't." When interviewed about the new style of comedy they were presenting, Eric said to a reporter, "Eddie's made me tougher and less gormless. I'm much harder towards Ernie now."

It is true, however, that Braben turned the vast majority of his attention to Ernie Wise. Again, the standard music hall performer – in Ernie's case, the know-it-all straight-man – was jettisoned for a softer, dreamier personality, which Braben brilliantly underscored by giving Ernie the pretension that he was the greatest writer "since wot Shakespeare wrote!" Not only would that create the vehicle for Ernie's "Plays wot he wrote" but also many a moment of supreme crosstalk with Eric, who forever has fun at Ernie's expense while, conversely, defending him against any guest star who doubts Ernie's literary claims.

With these new and quickly honed personalities installed, it seemed to us, the viewing public, as if those blurry ATV days of variety-hall comedy on television were a million years ago. Surely, the boys had always been like this, like the Eric and Ernie Braben had given us? Even my father, in these earliest times of the new-improved format, would occasionally still look at reel-to-reels (no videos, let alone DVDs back then) of the ATV shows and almost shake his head with disbelief. "I sounded so gormless back then," he remarked, doing a very good impression of himself from that era. And that was the biggest change of all. Hard as nails Ernie and gormless Eric mercifully had been jettisoned in favour of something much more sophisticated and in keeping with the new decade. In the Hills and Green format, Eric wouldn't have been allowed out on his own! And Ernie would have had few friends with his cruelty and arrogance. There would have been severe limitations on how far that original format could have run, but with the new set-up, the possibilities were endless.

The show very quickly developed in other ways. And I think that "the show", a personification of all they came to represent, quickly came to define what they were and still are. Previously, "the show" had been a grainy, 30-minute weekly skit starring Eric and Ernie, a vehicle for them on which to be funny. The colour shows, fully laden with guest stars, that they were now producing were far more than a mere vehicle for their talents.

Left A familiar bed scene with Eric and Ernie, but not from their television series. This was taken from their disappointing final film outing, *Night Train to Murder*, in 1984.

On top of this, Braben wanted them to share a bed – a throw back to the earliest days on the road staying in digs, and a great scenario for intimate cross-talk. Braben, astutely convinced an unconvinced Eric by pointing out that it had been good enough for Laurel and Hardy. Eric never lost his love for that particular double act, so agreed but added one extra idea of his own: he would more often than not be seen smoking a pipe in the bed. However unusual that might seem, he believed it would take any potential campness out of the sketches.

The bed sketches proved very popular with the viewing public. We all grew accustomed to Eric smoking his pipe and reading the *Dandy*, with Ernie either writing a play or reading the *Financial Times*. Just writing these words makes me realise how far they had now come during their relatively short association with Eddie Braben.

Coming hand-in-hand with the bed sketches were the flat sketches. These weren't so novel for Morecambe and Wise, who did a number of such routines with Hills and Green, but with Eddie Braben they became a fixture of every show, occasionally alternating with the bed sketches, and because of their more complete and *realistic* personalities, the flat created the subconscious notion that they really did live together!

What worked so well with these two new permanent comic fixtures was that they became a kind of sit-com within *The Morecambe and Wise Show* itself. Eric and Ernie never required a detailed storyline. Indeed, if you read one of their scripts cold, as I have often done, you start to wonder where the laughs are. Ultimately it is about *them* and not the material. So you have a flat sketch in which we come to imagine them living there and that we are no more than privileged listeners at the open door, peeping in perhaps to eavesdrop on snatches of their everyday life.

The whole process cannot have been that easy for Eddie. Not only was he the one dealing with the blank pieces of paper week-in, week-out, but also Eric always fell about laughing when he read anything Eddie wrote, only to become less enthusiastic the following day, having given it some reflection. Observers have remarked that it was probably out of embarrassment or due deference for Eddie that he never failed to deliver this initial over-enthusiasm. That might have been so, though I would say that my father often laughed loudly at things on television at home, then at the end of the show or film or sketch, say, "What a load of old cobblers!" which always made me chuckle. I think he was always searching for the genuinely funny moment in everything, and by laughing along with it perhaps felt he could encourage it to materialise.

It would be an error in this chapter on Morecambe and Wise's rise and rise as television stars to fail in giving a mighty nod of thanks to their producer, John Ammonds. Ammonds made everything gel, made any little problem go away, made any requested guest star appear. He pulled all the strings, and was more than worthy of a BAFTA or two for his quiet achievements.

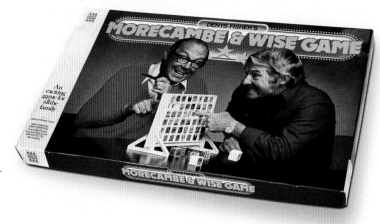

Needless to say, he didn't get one – that always goes to the obvious talent on the screen and not the hidden talent.

John was a mild-mannered man and a wonderful person to sit down with and reflect on those heady days when it must have felt as though they ruled the world. In the beginning, when Eric first worked for him in radio at the Manchester studios, Ammonds had great doubts that Morecambe and Wise would enjoy longevity as a double act. The more he saw of them, the more he realised he was wrong. As Ernie once put it, "The important thing is the team, the four of us – Eddie, the writer; Johnny Ammonds, the producer; and Eric and me."

And that combination led to two further glorious pleasures for their viewers: bigger and bigger guest stars, and their famed Christmas specials.

Top British households in the 1970s spent their Christmases watching the Morecambe and Wise Christmas Special – and playing their board game!

Above Morecambe and Wise won six BAFTAs between 1963 and 1973. They also received a posthumous Fellowship Award from the Academy in 1999.

Overleaf With Peter Cushing, their first major guest star at the BBC and then later their first guest star at Thames Television.

1966

THE MORECAMBE & WISE SHOW

starring
ERIC MORECAMBE

and ERNIE WISE

Two of a kind......

Above This ATV show card from 1966 is signed by Dick Hills and Sid Green who
worked as co-writers on the Morecambe & Wise series for ATV.

CHAPTER 8

The Christmas Glory Years

Ernie said, "People used to ask us how we managed to get all those big stars on the show, but I have to say that we never really had an answer for that." Ernie said it exactly as it was, and Eric had the same vague response to the same question, usually adding something like, "That's where the BBC has muscle." And he was right, because behind the scenes at the BBC, both Bill Cotton and John Ammonds were pretty relentless in securing names such as Laurence Olivier, John Mills, Shirley Bassey and André Previn, quietly presenting them to Morecambe and Wise in an "all in a day's work" sort of way. Mind you, the BBC did, and does, carry great global clout, and for Morecambe and Wise, losing it would prove to be one of the unfortunate side-effects of their departure to Thames Television in 1978.

Left The Grieg Piano Concerto, with André Previn in the 1971 Christmas show. It is now regarded as one of the greatest British comedy sketches of all time.

Above The perfect foil for Eric and Ernie, Previn returned to the fold for the 1972 and 1973 Christmas Specials, and, here, makes an appearance in an episode in September 1974.

While Peter Cushing is quite justly given the accolade of being Morecambe and Wise's first main guest star on their BBC shows, it is André Previn that was their biggest gamble. A maestro of his standing didn't normally do comedy, so making the initial approach was a daunting prospect. But when John Ammonds rang him, Previn at once told him what a wonderful show he thought *The Morecambe and Wise Show* was. Ammonds explained how pleased he was about that, "because I'm going to ask you to be on it".

Previn agreed at once, and without question one of Britain's finest moments of comedy entertainment was in development. My father said to me on Boxing Day 1971, the morning after the Previn Christmas show (which is how it is often described), "Whatever we do in the rest of our careers, at best we can only equal that. We won't be able to go any higher. That is the ceiling." And he was probably right, though making breakfast to "The Stripper" music arguably comes very close.

The journey between Previn agreeing and Previn appearing in a piece of comedy brilliance was a scary one for Morecambe and Wise and their production team. The problem was that Previn was working all around the world, and the customary minimum of five days rehearsal planned for him was a shock to his agent, who stated that it was categorically impossible. Eventually they agreed on three rehearsal days, which wasn't really much encouragement to Eric and Ernie.

And it got worse. Previn's mother fell ill out in the States, meaning he could only arrive the evening before the show was recorded. As Ammonds pointed out, "Eric tended to panic in that kind of situation...," but Ammonds was convinced that, as a routine, it was going to work. They just had to go with it.

Previn turned up at the studios claiming he had learned the script in the back of the taxi from the airport. Eric and Ernie were both highly sceptical about that.

"You can see in (Eric's) expression that he isn't quite sure whether it's all going to work or not," said Michael Grade, "because they are relying on a guest with whom they haven't had the chance to rehearse enough. If you watch that tape now, and I always watch for this moment, Eric visibly relaxes when André Previn exquisitely times that line of his: 'I'll go and get my baton – it's in Chicago', and it gets a huge belly laugh from the audience. (Eric's) face changes, and you can see him thinking, 'Boy, this is going to be good'...".

It's an interesting thought that over 40 years after that routine was performed, certainly in Britain, it is the one thing for which André Previn is universally remembered, despite his illustrious career as a conductor and composer. One can only sympathise with him when, arriving on a visit to London, he is greeted by a cabbie saying, "Where to, Mister Preview?"

During the 1970s, the number of guest stars not only increased with the growing expectation of the Morecambe and Wise

Christmas specials, but by the mid-seventies, with Ernest Maxin going from choreographer to producer and giving John Ammonds a well-deserved rest, they became altogether more musical. This was a specific demand of Eric and Ernie's – they loved doing the plays, the cross-talk, the flat and the bed routines, now they wanted to send up a bit of old Hollywood. This is why we were treated to the dancing newsreaders, Angela Rippon, Vanessa Redgrave, Elton John, Glenda Jackson, Hannah Gordon, Michelle Dotrice, Diana Rigg, Tom Jones and Shirley Bassey – even the actor Eric ("but I can't dance"!) Porter. To a greater or lesser degree, they all were involved musically with Morecambe and Wise.

Maxin said, "Whenever we went to discuss a new musical number, Eric would ask, 'Are we going to have the full Hollywood go this time, Ernest?' I would say, 'Yes, yes, Eric. You'll have all the moving cameras and everything.'"

The *Singin' in the Rain* parody is proof of that. Based faithfully on the original movie setting, but with the simple gag that although Eric, as the cop, gets soaking wet, it never once rains! A beautiful, yet simple, sideways tribute to a wonderful number. Not only does it remain Maxin's favourite, but also the star of the original film version, Gene Kelly, found it hilarious. He remarked that he had spent his life in the shadow of that great film, and was thrilled to see someone send it up so well.

Top left Eric with the actress Diana Rigg, during filming for the 1975 Christmas show. Diana Rigg described him as "very sexy".

Left A great example of one of their visual gags, with Eric using a television in a box and his glasses to good effect.

Top right Eric and Ernie with one of their most cherished guest stars, the former actress-turned-politician Glenda Jackson in a sketch about Queen Victoria.

Opposite above From a musical number with the singer John Hanson. One of my personal favourite moments prior to this sketch is when Hanson starts singing in his beautiful operatic voice, and Eric turns to him and says, "Get off! We don't want any of that rubbish on this show."

Opposite below "Nice to see you, to see you...nice." The indomitable Bruce Forsyth, a peer and personal friend of Eric and Ernie's.

1st Day.

Ernie

"BRING ME SUNSHINE"   MK 2!

SIR ALEC, ERIC AND ERN IN FRONT OF TABS.

IT NEVER SEEMS TO AMAZE ME.
How SO much LITTLE TALENT IS SUPPORTED

I THINK I'm DOING VERY WELL TONIGHT.
IT NEVER SEEMS TO AMAZE me How
SO much TALENT CAN BE SUPPORTED BY Such
LITTLE LEGS.

Left and opposite Ernie kept most of his Morecambe & Wise show scripts. This one is an extract from a sketch featuring the famed actor Sir Alec Guinness.

                    SIR ALEC WEARING OUTDOOR CLOTHING STANDING IN FRONT OF THE
                    CURTAINS AND LOOKING RATHER LOST. ERIC PEERING AT HIM THROUGH
                    GAP IN THE CURTAINS. SIR ALEC LOOKS AT HIS WRIST WATCH. ERIC.
                    ENTERS.

ERIC.   Yes?

SIR ALEC.   I'm waiting for Mr.Wise.

ERIC.   You're a bit early with the taxi, we haven't finished the show
                yet. If you'd be good enough to park your taxi around the back
                Mr.Wise will meet you when we've finished. We are doing a TV
                show with lots of famous people.
                    ERN LOOKING HORRIFIED THROUGH GAP IN CURTAINS.

SIR ALEC.   I erm ... I don't drive a taxi.

ERIC.   You can carry him home if you like but he is heavier than he
                looks
                    ERN QUICKLY THROUGH CURTAINS.   LOOK THRO.

ERN.   I do apologize most sincerely (TO ERIC) Don't you know who
                this is?

SIR ALEC.   My name is Guinness.

ERIC.   Stout fellow' (LAUGHING AT THIS)

ERN.   It really is most gracious of you to appear on our show, Sir
                Alec (ERN BOWS)

ERIC.   GASP OF ASTONISHMENT AS HE REALISES. I crave pardon, your
                Sirness' (ERIC BOWS)

SIR ALEC.   Gentlemen, please' I'll let you both into a little secret -
                it's always been a secret ambition of mine to appear in one
                of your comedy sketches.

ERN.   Gosh' Did you hear that, Eric.

ERIC.   Sir Alec, I give you my word, when we start doing comedy
                skecthes you'll be the first to know about it.

ERN.   We have got a comedy skecth for Sir Alec'

SIR ALEC.   I really am looking forward to it.

ERN.   Gosh' This way, please (INDICATES FOR SIR ALEC TO GO THROUGH
                CURTAINS)

SIR ALEC.   Thank you (HALF TURNS)

ERIC.   Ern' A bit of respect' That is Sir Alec

ERN.   (TO SIR ALEC) I do beg your pardon.
                    ERN TAKES HIS JACKET OFF AND PLACES IT DOWN FOR SIR ALEC TO
                    WALK ON. If you please?

ERIC.   I should think so
                    ERIC STEPS ONTO ERN'S JACKET, WIPES HIS FEET ON IT AND EXITS
                    THROUGH CURATINS.

ERN.   (EMBARRASSED) After you, Sir Alec.   ITEM 18

Top left A take on glam rock. Eric as aspiring pop star Spic Sparkle!

Top right With Vanessa Rednose (Redgrave) in a Napoleon and Josephine sketch from the 1973 Christmas show.

Below Ernie, sitting in an oversized chair, taking the weight off his "short, fat, hairy legs".

Opposite The duo dressed as nannies on a park bench during a 1976 episode for the BBC. The pair reprised the sketch seven years later, while at ITV. Eric looks the spitting image of his mother Sadie!

Ernie, who sang the number for the Morecambe and Wise version, was often asked if Gene Kelly's voice had been dubbed on it, which pleased him enormously.

By the mid-Seventies, Morecambe and Wise were living legends, and this could intimidate audiences. My father was always keen that he and Ernie not only had a warm-up man on the set (usually it was the actor-comedian Felix Bowness), but also that they did an extended warm-up of their own, just to reassure the audience that they were "on their side" as he put it.

"You could be greeted by awestruck faces," said Eric. "We wanted the laughs, so it was important to do a bit of business before the cameras were rolling." The material they did for the warm-ups was usually a piece taken from one of their "live" routines, developed over many years and toured nationwide as a live show in the Seventies. Their most frequent one was the Swiss slapping routine, which had become very popular in the Sixties for them, and invoked their more visual, fall-about comedy of that era. But I recall Charlie, the vent doll, making an occasional appearance, and it always went down a storm. Once the cameras were ready, so too was their audience.

Eric's health seemed in a good state now – indeed, when people asked how he was feeling these days, he had to think a moment about what they might mean!

Because of the repetition throughout that decade of their format, they did, by their own confession, begin to tire of doing the shows: not of the comedy or the partnership, but of that unchanging, almost regimented format that was both their Christmas show specials and annual series. They wanted to try something slightly different. Maybe a sit-com based solely around the bed and the flat routine. But they were, to a large extent, victims of their own success. The BBC and the viewing public were not looking for a new vehicle starring Morecambe

and Wise. They knew what they liked and it had been made plain in the recorded viewing figures (always around the 20 million mark) that what was wanted was more of the same. As Ernie put it, "Audiences will not accept us doing anything different." In a 1973 interview, Eric told the reporter, "We want to get away from doing the kind of stuff we've been doing so long."

They had a dalliance with a children's series called *Child's Play* and would crop up on rare occasions on other people's shows and in commercials – but that was about it outside their own work. The eagerness to discover new comic gold never came to fruition, and it was probably what ensured their enduring popularity. It required no effort from the public to understand in advance what they would be getting from the Morecambe and Wise brand. Add to that the fact that it was a family-friendly show and you have the makings of something special and universal.

What is interesting is that Eric and Ernie must have come to that conclusion for themselves, because their eagerness to find new goals in 1973 just about pre-dates their biggest Christmas outings – with the same, familiar, glorious format as ever.

One of the great moments of any show was the way in which Eric and Ernie engaged with their guests. As musician and actor Roy Castle put it, "It was an honour to go on a Morecambe and Wise show and be insulted." Which he did several times, sharing a

lifelong friendship with Eric and Ernie.

During this time, Eric and Ernie were in constant demand. I remember my father saying that sometimes he would get back from the studios, quickly change for some charity function and rush out of the house to reach the Dorchester, the Hilton, the Grosvenor or whichever hotel it was on that particular night, where he would bump straight into Ernie.

"I suppose I used to see much more of Eric socially than Ernie, because the curious thing was that Eric and Ernie didn't socialise much together," said the actor John Thaw. Thaw, with fellow actor Dennis Waterman, had been a guest for Eric and Ernie on their 1976 Christmas show. In return, they had them appear in the last ever episode of *The Sweeney*.

As Michael Grade put it, "Eric and Ernie worked hard at their professional relationship, but they simply didn't socialise together; didn't live in each other's pockets. And the simple reason for that was that they both had good marriages, different interests and different outlooks on life."

My mother, Joan, feels that the fact that they led separate lives away from their work doesn't warrant close examination. "What people forget about Eric and Ernie is that they were actually closer than husband and wife. They did so many shows together and really worked at those shows. This meant that they would see

each other every single day except weekends...." The BBC years continued to tick by, success after success, award after award (six from BAFTA alone). The Queen honoured them with OBEs, Eric put Luton Town FC on the map after becoming a director at the club, and Madame Tussauds immortalised them in wax.

On the domestic front, my brother, Steven, joined the Morecambe family in 1974 when Eric and Joan – understanding how fortunate in life they had been, and that their other two children had now grown up – adopted him from a nursing home where my sister, Gail, had been working. Ernie and Doreen were laying some foundations down in sunny Florida, which would remain an escape route for them throughout Ernie's life. Life in general continued throughout the Seventies in a Morecambe and Wise whirlwind, the intensity of which was tempered by a calming home life of relative domestic bliss. We lost Eric's mother, Sadie, in 1977 – George had collapsed and died the previous year, and with him had gone all of Sadie's interest in carrying on living. Ernie had lost his father, Harry, in 1966, and he comforted Eric on the loss of a parent, though Sadie's death was very painful for him, too. She had been as much a part of the Ernie Wise story as the Eric Morecambe one. I recall Ernie telling me that he and my father had had to work the night of his father's death in '66, and that they had gone out there with the old showbiz cry of "the show must go on" very much in their hearts. Because of work commitments, Ernie had only been able to manage to squeeze one

free day off for the funeral in Leeds. "Dad would have understood, though," recalled Ernie. "He would have known the pressures we were under and been proud we were so much in demand."

By the time Sadie died, Eric and Ernie were on a slightly more flexible timetable, which was especially fortunate for my father because I know that it took him a while to come to terms with losing his mother *and* the original driving force that had created his double act with Ernie.

In the latter stages of the 1970s there was nothing obvious for Morecambe and Wise to chase or to achieve. They had accepted the continued and permanent format of their shows, while still setting the bar in terms of quality television comedy shows. Our lives were generally very happy in this successful if, in its own way, mildly repetitive decade of series, Christmas shows and occasional family holidays. I recall my father saying that it doesn't matter how great your life is, "everything you do is still a

form of repetition". We were so fortunate as a family, yet perhaps something needed to be ignited; perhaps some kind of change really was required to avoid stagnation.

It came as little surprise to the family, therefore, when in January 1978 Eric and Ernie announced they were going to leave the BBC and move to Thames Televsion. Philip Jones was then Head of Light Entertainment at Thames. Jones had been in contact with Morecambe and Wise since their first meeting in Blackpool during the 1950s, and remained a close personal friend of Ernie and Doreen's.

"I often thought how great it would be if Eric and Ernie would join us at Thames," he said, "but I never mentioned anything because it would have been wrong to let that intrude on our social lives..."

The then managing director at Thames, Bryan Cowgill, was a huge Morecambe and Wise fan and took the wish a step further. A lunch was arranged for Eric and Ernie and their agent, Billy Marsh. Jones admitted to serenading the double act into joining them at Thames.

This was all particularly tough on their friend and current employer at the BBC, Bill Cotton. To say he was devastated by their departure is to put it mildly. My father swore to his last day that they had in no way meant to upset Cotton, whom they loved and respected. Ernie agreed, and pointed out that leaving the BBC was purely a business matter. They did, however, leave Bill Cotton high and dry on this occasion, and he wasn't even in the country at the time to talk them out of the proposed move.

Decades on, after countless discussions with other celebrities and backroom people of that era, it is clear that the general consensus – and one held in the Morecambe household, too – is that the move to Thames was not the right thing to have done. It was as unreasonable to Bill Cotton as when writers Dick Hills and Sid Green left Morecambe and Wise following Eric's heart attack, but it was also unreasonable to expect Thames to be able to compete with the BBC's clout and history. Entertainment folklore has it that they moved to Thames for better money. That was not so. They had plenty of money as the BBC's top entertainers. And they were no longer looking for a fresh format. Indeed, Thames explained early on that they simply wanted to buy the whole BBC show exactly as it was. They wanted to own exactly what the nation's viewing public so clearly enjoyed.

The carrot for Eric and Ernie – the single reason they deserted ship – was Thames' offer (on top of the whole basic deal) to help them make a big-screen movie. This was utterly irresistible for Eric and Ernie, who felt they had only scratched the surface of movie making while doing the Rank films in the mid-Sixties. Eric had this dream of him and Ernie doing something cinematically

global in the way Peter Sellers had with the "Panther" movies. I always felt that was a little ambitious and even naïve. It was the equivalent of saying that Sellers could do an annual television Christmas special, which would be brilliant and draw in around 25 million viewers. An element of "stick to what you do best" would have been the sensible approach here, but when you have an unfulfilled ambition *and* you are being courted, sticking to anything sensible becomes difficult.

Comedian, presenter and writer Paul Merton told me of a conversation he had with Bill Cotton some time after Eric's death, suggesting that Morecambe and Wise were seriously thinking of returning to the BBC by 1984 (the year Eric died). There was a quiet air in the Morecambe house during 1983 and '84 that suggested Eric and Ernie would persevere with Thames, but that it wasn't to be the company with which they would end their careers. The impression that a door to the BBC remained open became a more solid idea with each passing month. My father never knocked Thames or referred to a move back to the BBC but, following what would prove to be their last ever Christmas show (1983), it was easy to sense that something had to change. That vein of pleasure that had always flowed through their careers, even in the tough times, had suddenly gone.

My father certainly looked to us for reassurance whenever a Thames show transmitted. "It was good, though, don't you think?" was often asked, and this from a man who was previously so self-assured with the work he and Ernie were doing at the BBC, that he never normally asked what we thought at all; we simply told him ourselves. It was a difficult question to answer, for as much as I genuinely enjoyed what they did for Thames, I couldn't help but compare it to the BBC years.

Nature's ageing process was also playing a part. Ernie's hair had gone from grey to white, and Eric switched from the dark-brown, horn-rimmed glasses for which he had so long been famed to a tortoise shell pair, giving him the air of jovial archivist.

The Thames shows were never bad, but the production values and general guest-star pulling power of Thames was never in the same league as the BBC. This gave their shows more of a "Benny Hill" quality, which just didn't suit their particular talents or style. It was reminiscent of the Rank films that they did. Horses for courses had clearly gone out the window. There were more jokey props and physical silliness, which worked all right, but lacked the clever crosstalk that had dominated Morecambe and Wise's work since they appeared on stage at the Liverpool Empire in August 1941. And however much we loved the likes of Jill Gascoine, Isla St Clair, Gemma Craven, Peter Vaughan and Suzanne Danielle, they weren't Shirley Bassey, Tom Jones, Sir John Gielgud, André Previn or Laurence Olivier.

Above "Not now Arthur!" Harmonica player Arthur Tolcher was a childhood friend of Eric and Ernie and he was a running gag on their show.

Below Cliff Richard pays a visit to Eric and Ernie's flat in January 1973. But I don't think the duo quite know who he is!

Opposite In the navy with Cliff Richard in the same show. After dancing with mops, they performed an hilarious tap dance with metal buckets.

as well as that year's Christmas show.

I know that when they eventually started to do more shows at Thames from 1980 onwards, Eric and Ernie began to feel there was a paucity of decent material for them to work with. In fact, they resorted to rehashing old routines they had done at the BBC, even going right back to their ATV material. There was nothing to be gained by the rehash, and I personally felt, and still feel, it was a very, very bad decision to go down that particular route. They would have been better to have employed writers with a directive saying they wanted *similar* ideas to those older shows, but essentially set in fresh scenarios. They could even have limited their screen appearances – rarefied themselves a little, as the comedian Rowan Atkinson put it to me at that time. That would have enhanced the excitement for each of their shows.

But the biggest problem Morecambe and Wise had at Thames was Eric's failing health. No sooner had the first shows been rehearsed, recorded and transmitted, than Eric collapsed from a second heart attack early one morning in March 1979 while opening the fridge at his Hertfordshire home. He fell backwards on top of me. I was about two feet away, dressed and ready to catch the train to London for work. At first I thought he was messing around as there was something

On top of that, writer Eddie Braben and producer John Ammonds didn't make the initial move to Thames with them. Their own BBC contract had another year or two to complete. When one considers how much great work they had all achieved as a team of four, this sudden halving of the unit must have felt very peculiar, and left Eric and Ernie feeling somewhat isolated and vulnerable. My memory of this time is that Eric and Ernie didn't know in advance of signing their new contracts for Thames that Braben and Ammonds would not be able to join them at the outset. The writing team of Barry Cryer and John Junkin was drafted in to create material for 1978's hour-long Thames special

amusing and surreal about the moment. He was wearing his pyjamas and dressing gown: a distinct hint, I thought, of their making breakfast to "The Stripper" music, which had become a classic routine from their show.

"I think I'll be all right in a minute," he said. But he didn't look all right to me. My mother was in bed with a broken ankle, which added to the drama. We called the doctor, and both he and an ambulance arrived very swiftly. Off went my father to St Albans' hospital, where he recovered, but not without an eventual diagnosis recommending that he would need by-pass surgery.

It was an inauspicious start to their Thames career, but one

completely out of their hands and everyone at Thames was fantastically kind to them both, sympathetic and tolerant. There was never a sense of pressure being brought to bear upon them.

Meanwhile, and just prior to this drama, the BBC had started repeating *The Best Of Morecambe and Wise* at the BBC, which was both clever yet obvious when considered. They had such a wonderful source of material, and Thames had very little. So far, so bad! The saving grace in this entire charade was the love that the British public had and continued to have for Morecambe and Wise.

The surgery, relatively commonplace nowadays but still in its infancy in 1979, was carried out by Professor Magdi Yacoub at Harefield hospital. It was fascinating for me when putting this book together to discover that my father had kept a page of thoughts, written in the early hours of the morning just prior to his life-saving operation, expressing how he felt about what might be (*see* the facsimiles).

The operation was considered a great success, and my father returned home less worried about Morecambe and Wise, although he was acutely aware they had made a fresh commitment to a different television corporation who had thus far received very little product from them.

Their Thames Christmas show of 1979, their only new show that year, became an interview with David Frost with a few easy comedy ideas – including a sight gag with Glenda Jackson involving rising stools – and various excellent old clips thrown in.

Above The 1976 Christmas show, starring Dennis Waterman and John Thaw. The treat for Eric and Ernie was that Waterman and Thaw got them back on their own show – *The Sweeney* – for the last ever episode two years later. Eric claimed he had more fun with that than anything they had done before.

Opposite One of Eric and Ernie's most revered and best remembered sketches, Anthony and Cleopatra. Here they are seen doing a Wilson, Keppel and Betty sand dance routine with Glenda Jackson.

What's extraordinary to me is that by 1980, a year after Eric's heart operation, it was almost a case of "as you were". Morecambe and Wise were at the studios planning a new series for Thames. I'm fairly certain that had he and Ernie not felt hugely obliged to Thames as their new and friendly employer, they would not have been discussing a new series and Christmas shows, but possible retirement instead. Obviously, this decision would have been largely based on my father's deteriorating health during those Thames years, but that wouldn't have been the only reason. Eric Morecambe, during his recuperation period, had now developed a massive interest away from his partnership with Ernie. It had come from out of the blue, but it had affected him so much that he referred to it as his new or second career. And he claimed it gave him more personal fulfilment than anything he had done or achieved as a comedian.

He was about to become a novelist.

CHAPTER 9

All Things Must Pass

It was fascinating how Eric's love for writing books, which had begun after an unexpected meeting and conversation with a publisher called Christopher Falkus (then running Eyre Methuen) enthused him so much that he began to see writing as an alternative future to comedy. Indeed, he quickly became less eager to return to comedy at all. I recall him saying at this time that he didn't even *want* to be funny, and watching comedy no longer interested him in the slightest.

Below This photo shows the real effort that went into each and every moment of their shows, particularly rehearsals for the musical numbers.

The first book Eric tackled during his recuperation period, and the one that would set him up against his own career as a comedian, was *Mr Lonely*. The book was erroneously assumed to be autobiographical, but he would in fact save *that* idea for his next novel. *Mr Lonely* was certainly the story of a male comedian, but that is where any similarity with Eric ceased. He deliberately made his main protagonist a club stand-up comic of dubious morality and questionable comic material to lay down clear divisions between himself and his literary anti-hero. The media's insistence that it was somehow autobiographical therefore came as a bit of surprise to him.

While *Mr Lonely* is not an astounding piece of fiction, I know that his fans have a great love for the book, because Eric and his humour exist on each and every page. On re-reading it again quite recently, I too could feel him at my shoulder, smiling at all his own little observations and the gags that he had put into the story and the characters. It was truly like Eric was alive again.

But the book is also quite a dark comedy, which surprised me as much as anyone. I think it benefits from that – it takes us out of the expected into the unexpected. I know for sure that whenever he did promotional interviews for this first work of fiction, gone was the mischievous comedian: this was Eric Morecambe the *novelist*. That was how he wished to present himself and all he wanted to talk about. When any of the interviews moved on to discuss his partnership with Ernie and future Morecambe and Wise shows, there was a hint of teeth gritting as he tried to muster appropriate enthusiasm. It really wasn't something for which he was feeling properly enthusiastic any longer.

His on-going health issues, including the heart by-pass surgery, had at first frustrated him when he thought about returning to his partnership with Ernie, but they were now almost welcomed as a lengthy and enforced reprieve.

Above Away from the television studios Eric enjoyed many hobbies, including bird watching, fishing and photography.

Opposite He was the butt of many gags, but Des O'Connor was in reality one of Eric and Ernie's best friends in showbiz.

It is hard to know what Ernie Wise might have been thinking at this time. In prime physical shape and ready to get back to work on their double act, he was certainly aware that his partner was engaged in producing his first book during his recovery period, but how much he knew of Eric's increasing disinterest in comedy, I really don't know. Possibly very little, because Eric and Ernie tended to stand by each other and were very defensive and protective of one another. I cannot envisage my father ever saying directly to Ernie that he wanted to end their partnership. Indeed, even when he was absolutely sure, a year or two later, that that was the correct and healthier option for them, he never could bring himself to have that conversation in full, though he did allude to it just once. Many years later, in an interview, Ernie recalled a moment in a dressing room at that time when Eric vaguely alluded to the idea they might call it a day and end the partnership. Ernie replied that he must choose to do what he felt was best. And as it was neither a wholly direct question nor a definitive answer, the obvious outcome was that *nothing* changed.

Eric's recovery was slow, but Eric and Ernie inevitably re-committed to Thames and a number of shows, both the series and Christmas specials, while Eric's writing continued in the background, mostly at randomly grabbed opportunities.

On its publication, *Mr Lonely* was well received, and Eric began writing a second novel called *Stella*, making a gentle but significant start before putting it to one side to try his hand at a children's book. Stella was a novel destined to be published

posthumously, and I would have the great honour of completing it on his behalf in 1985 following his death the previous year. At the time of writing, I am working with Bob Golding, who starred in and toured with the play *Morecambe* (more on that in the following chapter) and two talented writer-actresses to turn the book into a small touring stage play.

Vampires had always fascinated my father, from Bram Stoker's original novel, to Hollywood's Bela Lugosi and the Hammer House of Horrors Christopher Lee films, and it was to these mythical creatures of the night that his literary interest now turned. *The Reluctant Vampire* and then *Vampire's Revenge* took up much of his time spent away from the studios, though every now and then he would return to *Stella*, though he admitted that, unlike *Mr Lonely*, he was finding the story line problematic.

But it was still the television studios – albeit those at Teddington Lock rather than the more familiar ones of BBC TV Centre – to which Eric and Ernie would trundle along with surprising repetitiveness, considering how dire Eric's health had so recently been. It's all very easy to realise with hindsight, but at this time someone should have said "enough is enough". After all, they had

4.55. A.M.   HAREFIELD HOSPITAL.

I'm SUPRISED HOW CALM I FEEL.
CONSIDERING MY TEMPERATURE IS 115 -
MY BLOOD PRESSURE IS 206 OVER
200 - AND MY PULSE RATE IS
192 A MINUTE - MONDAY MORNING
EARLY - JUNE 25 79. THE BIRDS
LIKE DES O'CONNER, HAVE JUST STOPPED
SINGING - THE CONDEMNED MAN ATE
A HEARTY VALIUM, AND THE
BRAVEST WORDS I CAN THINK OF ✱ARE
TWO WORDS ✱
                THE GREEKS HAVE A WORD
FOR IT, THE FRENCH HAVE A MOVEMENT
FOR IT, AND I'M SURE THE AMERICANS
HAVE AN ICE CREAM NAMED AFTER
IT. BUT AS AN ENGLISHMAN, I CAN
ONLY SAY - 'I HOPE I'VE GOT THE
HEART FOR IT.

THE VARIETY CLUB
OF GREAT BRITAIN

IN RECOGNITION
OF THE SUPPORT
GIVEN BY

Ernie Wise OBE

TO VARIETY CLUB
IN ITS WORK FOR SICK,
HANDICAPPED, ORPHANED
AND DEPRIVED CHILDREN
THROUGHOUT
THE UNITED KINGDOM

Chief Barker
Variety Club of Great Britain

Above left Eric, Ernie and wives with Mike Winters (of Mike and Bernie Winters) in Florida in the early 1980s.

Above right Eric and Ernie's headgear bemuses Roy Castle during a Thames show in November 1982.

Right With showbiz pal Max Bygraves, who didn't appear in *The Morecambe and Wise Show* until 1981.

been a working act since they were both young teenagers in 1940.

The general opinion is that they were still as dedicated to their art as ever, but it is undeniable that there was a spark missing from Eric and a tautness in Ernie's demeanour that suggested they shouldn't still be doing this work. Comedy, and sitting at the top of the comedy tree, is very stressful and very precarious. The old line about there being only one way to go and it isn't up, was now clearly haunting the boys.

Personally, I concluded that they simply didn't think about analysing their situation at all – they were too busy being in the moment, and performing comedy was what they had always done; it was all they knew to do. Also, they were thrilled to have the old team back together, with producer John Ammonds and scriptwriter Eddie Braben having now made the move from the BBC to Thames. I feel that the shows benefited from the team's reunion, though a lacklustre air, related directly to Eric's long run of ill health and the fact that both men had aged somewhat since their glory days of the BBC, would always prevent a return to the top of their game. There was the sneaking suspicion that they, and all who worked with them, knew it.

It can't have been easy for Eric and Ernie to exist together in this strange bubble where everything was all right, but never as it once had been. Eric had once said in an interview, "Ours is a relationship based on genuine friendship, and a mutual admiration. We both think the other is the funniest man breathing!" I sensed at this time that that belief in each other was being sorely tested. While we knew deep down that their glory days were now behind them, everyone believed that Eric's health

Above Between takes with their producer and long-time friend John Ammonds. Like Eddie Braben, Johnny was a pivotal member of that small, tight group that reinvented Morecambe and Wise and took them to new heights at the BBC.

Below Behind the scenes at an early Thames television rehearsal.

was on the mend. What we didn't realise was that he was actually dying from heart disease, and quite quickly.

However reduced the pleasure in still performing as a double act, it would have frightened them to have stopped something that had begun when they were children. The boys almost needed Sadie back to advise them – or even just to give them a kick up the backside to encourage them to take a difficult decision. That was, perhaps, more her style!

Meanwhile, Thames Television's film arm, Euston Films, was obligated to honour Morecambe and Wise's contract with a big screen outing, the temptation that had been the deciding factor in the double act's decision to switch channels. Despite that being the case, Thames had very little appetite for the project, and it is abundantly clear that, although it made a useful carrot to lure the boys away from the BBC, they were never going to invest a great amount of time, effort, creative thought and money into the project. It was merely a fulfillment of their contractual duties.

The film that Morecambe and Wise eventually completed not that many months before Eric's sudden death was *Night Train to Murder*. From the aficionado's perspective, it is a useful and appreciated part of Morecambe and Wise's large canon. Paul Jenkinson, who runs the excellent Morecambe and Wise website, has had many discussions with me over the merits of the film, and Paul is a serious expert and connoisseur when it comes to this double act.

From a moviemaker's and general viewer's perspective, it is a fairly creaky, cheap, turgid and not that funny film. Yet there is something in that last scene of Eric and Ernie walking off into the sunset holding hands in that 1930s Chaplinesque/Laurel-and-Hardy Hollywood fashion that brings a lump to my throat.

Ernie was always good at accepting the ups and the downs for what they were, but Eric was poleaxed when finally he got to see the finished movie. "It wasn't what we set out to do!" he moaned after the private screening. But what depressed him the most was that he hadn't noticed at the time they were shooting it that it wasn't right. Which is very strange, as my father was a man who was very in tune with every facet of Morecambe and Wise, from script to gags to performance. He even had a shrewd eye on lighting and camera angles. This slip-up on his behalf was accompanied by several others at that time, and we later came to learn that it was quite common in cases of extreme heart disease for the brain not to function as well as it should – for rational decision-making to become an issue.

Eric insisted on the film being "lost" and, sure enough, it never went out until after his death. It eventually received a

transmission during children's television scheduling, and was sold (with a surprising positive response, ironically) to various European countries.

Eric was also doing some independent filming. He appeared in Charles Wallace's John Betjeman short films, with Betjeman himself narrating his own poems and Eric as part of a decent cast that included Beryl Reid and John Alderton. He also worked with Wallace on a short film with Tom Baker called *The Passionate Pilgrim* in which Eric is surprisingly spritely and, as a piece of work, it has remained very popular with his fans.

The last Morecambe and Wise Christmas show appeared in 1983. It was very weak by their own high standards, relying for too heavily on material from past shows, some even as far back as their days on the variety tours. The paucity of decent material had long been a thorn to both comedians. Had Eric lived, it might have been this singular fact and nothing else that encouraged them finally to close the book on their working act.

In May 1984, while doing a Q-and-A evening for Stan Stennett, an old pal from Eric and Ernie's variety halls days, at Stan's Roses Theatre in Tewkesbury, Eric left the stage at the end of the show

Top Taken at Teddington Studios, this is a team photo of the cast and crew of Thames TV's *Morecambe and Wise Show*.

Centre Eric and Ernie alongside Nigel Hawthorne and Patricia Brake, their only two guests from the Thames TV episode broadcast on 8 December 1982.

Bottom Eric and Nigel Hawthorne wait for action in a sketch titled "Lost Legionnaires" (or should that be "Lost in Thought Legionnaires") from 8 December 1982.

Opposite With fellow Thames TV starlet, Benny Hill. Hill's international appeal was extraordinary. His show ran in some capacity from 1955 until 1991 and aired in 140 countries.

to a standing ovation, and collapsed in the wings. He died in the early hours of 28 May at Cheltenham General Hospital. Ernie would feel bad forever afterwards about not having been with his partner that evening, as it was so rare that they worked alone. The Morecambe and Wise double act had finally come to an end, but not in the manner anyone had envisaged.

Ernie Wise had lost his greatest friend and his job in one fell swoop as a nation went into mourning for a man who had become everyone's favourite uncle.

At home in Harpenden, Hertfordshire, we the family were trying to come to terms with what had happened, while simultaneously facing the media mayhem that his passing had created. Grieving for his loss would be denied us for some weeks – months, even – until the papers had found other headlines and stories to take their interest. And then, as quickly as they had descended, the reporters were gone.

Ernie did his round of media work, talking about his life with Eric, while deflecting ideas of him carrying on either on his own as a solo comic – not possible, he announced – or as a double act. There was a notion to link him with comedian Eric Sykes, so that there would still be an Eric and Ernie partnership. But I know that Ernie found that both pointless and tasteless, and surely Eric Sykes concurred. So, for a short time, Ernie and his wife Doreen disappeared to their place in Florida while they, too, came to terms with the fact that the most amazing of journeys – a tale of rags-to-riches, if you will – had finally come to an end.

Ernie re-emerged the following year with something more akin to a smile on his face, and looking a little whiter, thinner and older. In 1986, he took a one-man show to Australia. It was a tour of Q and As blended with stories of his and Eric's past, plus clips of their shows. As much as anything, it was a nostalgic return to the country that had kept their double act together in 1958 when a lack of work seemed poised to bring about its demise. Once that "wrapped" and he was back in the UK, he virtually disappeared other than making the occasional breakfast and afternoon television chat show appearance.

His only other notable outings were in the long-running farce *Run For Your Wife*, a few television panel games and pantos, and a wordy role in the unfinished Dickens work *The Mystery of Edwin Drood*, which hit London's West End in 1987 and co-starred the singer Lulu.

I met up with Ernie several times during the early 1990s, finding him very together, much more bubbly than those first five or six years following his partner's death, very friendly and keen to chat about the past. He seemed less in a hurry to achieve anything, and after a bout of poor health, including a series of mini strokes, he announced his retirement in the mid-Nineties. He told me that all his life he had been plagued with breathing difficulties when working in theatres, which, coming from a man who had spent much of his working life treading the boards, was a big surprise to me.

In March 1999, Ernie died at the relatively young age of 73.

We were all a little shocked that he had succumbed to strokes and heart problems, as Ernie had been the stalwart figure of the double act; the one never to have suffered even a cold during the Morecambe and Wise heyday. There is a part of me that forever will be convinced that Eric's *very* premature death at the age of just 58 had a much more profound affect on Ernie than was perhaps understood or appreciated at the time. It would be going too far to say that Eric's sudden death took away his reason for living; that he died from a broken heart – Ernie was a bubbly, friendly man with a happy marriage to Doreen, and all the money he could possibly want – but it would be reasonable to say that he never fully recovered from the loss of his partner. That definitely would have had an impact on his health. As he said, there was always a cold draught down one side where Eric used to be.

On a personal level, with Ernie always at the end of a phone for me to talk about their early days on the road, about my father's mischievousness and boyhood pranks, and many, many other nostalgic recollections and images, it wasn't until he died that for me Morecambe and Wise became something to be referred in the past tense. They had still existed as something in the present moment to me until that point.

The biggest surprise of all, something even Ernie would have not expected, is that fourteen years after his own death, Morecambe and Wise are still ticking on, and very much part of the nation's psyche.

Top A rose between two thorns. The ever lovely Joanna Lumley takes part in Eric and Ernie's version of *Thoroughly Modern Millie* in October 1981.

Above A Royal show for HRH Prince Charles. Far left is the co-chairman of the Combined Charities Commission, Andrew Neatrour; next to him is Eric and Ernie's agent, Billy Marsh.

Opposite Eric returns to Harefield Hospital, Middlesex, where he had had life-saving surgery performed by Professor Magdi Yacoub in June 1979. Whether this is a stunt photo, or if all the nurses were this attractive is not certain!

CHAPTER 10

The Remarkable Legacy

The Morecambe and Wise story following the deaths of Eric and Ernie has been almost as remarkable as during their working lifetime.

Above A programme from the hugely successful David Pugh/Kenneth Branagh 2002 production, *The Play What I Wrote*.

Left As big stars, Morecambe and Wise were always in demand. Here, they attend the opening of a new Allders store (with some enthusism it appears!).

BAFTAs, many documentaries, countless screenings of their shows and even a series of new ones based around lost and rare material have kept the Morecambe and Wise phenomenon rolling on. There has been a series based around their musical numbers, two plays, a fictional film of their early years starring, and created by, Victoria Wood and, most wonderful of all, a statue of each man in their home towns of Morecambe and Leeds. Eric's statue on the front at Morecambe Bay is particularly spectacular as sculptor Graham Ibbeson was given a large area to display his work. This resulted in the bronze statue standing on a grand, circular platform that is covered with all the names of Morecambe and Wise's guest stars, many of their best-known expressions and the lyric to "Bring Me Sunshine". Personally, I think it is unfortunate that the stone statue of Ernie Wise in Leeds was not also done in bronze. He is worthy of something better, and there has been a growing interest in the idea of joint bronze statues of the two comedians side by side forever, location as yet undecided.

David Pugh produced the first Morecambe-and-Wise-related play in 2002 – *The Play What I Wrote* – with Kenneth Branagh directing. Written and performed by the Right Size (Sean Foley

and Hamish McColl) with additional material by Eddie Braben, and the Olivier award-winning actor, as he would become in this production, Toby Jones, as well as yours truly as script consultant, it toured in four different productions over several years, also appearing on Broadway. It was as near-perfect a sideways tribute to Morecambe and Wise as you could get, the premise of the tale being that Sean and Hamish are doing a tribute to Morecambe and Wise, but Hamish (who is the equivalent of the straight-man) doesn't know that that's what they are doing. Guest stars then appear – different ones for virtually each performance, which is very Morecambe and Wise in style – creating an amusing and somewhat manic show that links to the present as well as reflecting on the "golden age" of entertainment.

For Kenneth Branagh, directing the play was a dream come true. "When I was 14, I wrote to Morecambe and Wise for tickets for one of their television shows," he said. "The letter that came back was one of the first ever addressed to me at my house. It had BBC stamped at the top of the envelope, and as I ran downstairs to collect it, my brother, who was in particularly bullying mode at the time, was so completely intrigued, that he opened it.

"Inside was a signed photograph. And although there were no tickets left, and I never got to see Morecambe and Wise live, I still have the photo to this day."

One of the most interesting observations Ken made to me was when he pointed out that all the great comics have a sing-song voice, delivering their lines almost musically. This is so spot on that it has staggered me ever since that I had never previously noticed it for myself.

The second play, which was produced for the 2009 Edinburgh Festival, was a virtuoso one-man show, a whistle-stop tour through the life of Eric Morecambe, called simply *Morecambe*, written and performed by Bob Golding. When the likes of Ronnie Corbett ring up suggesting you have to see how good it is, you know that it must be a bit special.

Victoria Wood's film of Morecambe and Wise's early days, screened in January 2001 and titled *Eric and Ernie*, was as moving as Golding's play, if a little more fictionalised. Victoria played Eric's mother, Sadie. As with both the plays that came before it, *Eric and Ernie* picked up an award: it was a BAFTA for Daniel Rigby who quite superbly portrayed the adult Eric, and he edged out Matt Smith for *Doctor Who* and Benedict Cumberbatch for his excellent portrayal of Sherlock Holmes in the BBC series *Sherlock*.

The game continues. In 2012, there were various, if slightly quirky at times, Morecambe and Wise appearances. The BBC's Children In Need evening had Eric and Ernie as holograms singing their signature tune "Bring Me Sunshine" accompanied by radio's Chris Moyles. There are many other projects afoot that involve Morecambe and Wise, although I am not at liberty to announce

Above left Eric and Ernie at a charity dinner for veterans of the Falklands War at the Royal Garden Hotel, Kensington.

Above right Ernie appears in the West End production of *The Mystery of Edwin Drood*, following his partner, Eric's, death. The cast consisted of Ernie, Lulu, Julia Hills, David Burt and Mark Ryan.

Right A smaller version of the bronze statue of Eric that can be seen on the front in his home town of Morecambe.

Below left This frying pan prop was found in Eric's office. The bacon turns into a smile with teeth!

Opposite The inimitable Eric Morecambe and Ernie Wise.

them, and I know that fans will be very pleased with the boys' ongoing mainstream appearances.

On a personal level, I am hoping to collaborate on a project with Bob Golding involving Eric's novel, *Stella*, which I completed. Since the play, *Morecambe*, Bob has become a family friend.

I think Eric and Ernie would have been delighted and shocked in equal measures at the way in which their reputations have continued to grow, at the position they hold as the nation's best-loved comedy duo and at the pleasure they still bring to millions. I know my father remarked that he saw himself and Ernie as one day being a cult interest thing, and he told my sister, Gail, that she should continue to watch the shows after he was dead and gone otherwise "it will have all been for nothing". Like us all, he

underestimated the sheer quality of their work, and the love of a nation that so looks forward to watching them each and every Christmas.

Perhaps there is a part of all of us that is surprised, but when you remember that you are talking not just about two very funny gentlemen, but two very funny gentle men, it is easier to understand in these harder, tougher times, from where this love and affection emanates.

Bring me sunshine, in your smile,

Bring me laughter, all the while,
In this world where we live,
There should be more happiness,
So much joy you can give,
To each brand new bright tomorrow.

Make me happy, through the years,
Never bring me any tears,
Let your arms be as warm as the sun from up above,
Bring me fun, bring me sunshine, bring me love.

Chronology

1925
Ernest Wiseman born, 27 November. One of five children.

1926
John Eric Bartholomew born, 14 May. Only child.

1931
Age six, Ernie joins his father, Harry, on stage at working men's clubs as a double act called Carson and Kid.

1936
Eric joins cousin Peggy at Miss Hunter's dancing school in Morecambe.

1938
Eric leaves school aged 12 to pursue a career in show business. Ernie appears on stage at Morley's New Pavilion Theatre.

1939
Eric wins a talent competition organised by *The Melody Maker*. Auditions for impresario Jack Hylton in Manchester. Encounters Ernie Wise for the first time, but they do not have the opportunity to speak.

Ernie appears with Arthur Askey in the little comedian's show *Band Waggon*, at the London Palladium.

1941
Eric and Ernie appear as a double act for the very first time at the Liverpool Empire Theatre. Eric changes his name to Eric Morecambe.

1943
Eric and Ernie appear in the smash-hit London show, *Strike a New Note*, and make their first radio appearance in *Youth Must Have Its Fling*.

1944
Ernie is called up for war service in the Merchant Navy, Eric is sent down the mines in Accrington as a Bevin Boy.

1945
Eric is invalided out of the mines with poor health and slight heart problems.

1946
Eric and Ernie reunite after a chance meeting in London's Regent Street.

1947
Morecambe and Wise tour in *Lord John Sanger's Circus and Variety Tour*.

Top Eric and Ernie in the first year of their double act looking very natty with their boaters.

Below Someone or something is making them smile as they pose for a publicity shot.

Left Eric and Ernie publicise one of their theatre shows at the seaside.

Below A happy pair pose with one of their six BAFTA awards.

1950
Morecambe and Wise sign with the agent Frank Pope and begin appearing regularly in Moss Empire theatres.

1951
Morecambe and Wise make their television debut on the *Parade of Youth*.

1952
Eric marries Joan Bartlett.

1953
Ernie marries Doreen Blythe.

A daughter, Gail, is born to Eric and Joan.

954
Morecambe and Wise's first television series for the BBC, *Running Wild*, is a flop.

1956
A son, Gary, is born to Eric and Joan.

Morecambe and Wise return to television, guesting on Winifred Atwell's shows. The scripts are written by Johnny Speight.

1958
Morecambe and Wise tour Australia.

1960
Morecambe and Wise change agents, joining Billy Marsh.

1961
Morecambe and Wise return to presenting their own television series for Lew Grade at ATV.

Morecambe and Wise are invited to appear on a Royal Command Performance.

1963
Morecambe and Wise win the first of six BAFTAs.

1964
The Beatles are guest stars on The Morecambe and Wise Show. Morecambe and Wise make their first trip to New York to guest on *The Ed Sullivan Show*.

The first of three Morecambe and Wise films for cinematic release – *The Intelligence Men* – is filmed at Pinewood Studios.

1965
The second Morecambe and Wise film – *That Riviera Touch* – is filmed at Pinewood and on location in the South of France.

1966
The third Morecambe and Wise film – *The Magnificent Two* – is filmed at Pinewood Studios.

1968
Morecambe and Wise smash all records in summer season at Great Yarmouth and leave ATV to join the BBC.

In November, Eric suffers the first of three heart attacks.

1969
Eric makes full recovery and Morecambe and Wise continue to make television shows. They win a BAFTA award. Eddie Braben becomes their new scriptwriter replacing Dick Hills and Sid Green.

1970
Morecambe and Wise win another BAFTA award.

1971
André Previn, Shirley Bassey and Glenda Jackson all make highly publicised debuts on *The Morecambe and Wise Show*.

The pair win another BAFTA award and are honoured by the Radio Industries Organisation.

1972
The duo receive a fifth BAFTA award.

1973
A sixth BAFTA award.

Morecambe and Wise publish their autobiography *Eric and Ernie* from interviews put together with ghost writer Dennis Holman.

1974
Honoured by the Variety Club and the Water Rats.

1976
Both are awarded the OBE and the Freedom of the City of London. Eric is awarded an honorary degree by the University of Lancaster.

1977
The Morecambe and Wise Christmas Show is watched by a record viewing figure of 28 million.

1978
Morecambe and Wise join Thames Television. Former Prime Minister Harold Wilson is the guest star on their first Christmas show.

The pair receive a Variety Club award.

1979
In January, Eric suffers second heart attack. Undergoes by-pass surgery.

1980
Eric writes his first novel, *Mr Lonely*, while recovering from heart by-pass surgery.

1981
Morecambe and Wise voted into the TV Hall of Fame.

1983
Morecambe and Wise's very last Christmas show is transmitted.

1984
Morecambe and Wise complete their film for Euston Films, *Night Train to Murder*, destined to be their last work together.

Eric dies on 28 May at the Roses Theatre, Tewkesbury.

1985

Eric's second novel, *Stella*, is completed by Gary Morecambe and published by Severn House.

Ernie Wise makes the first ever mobile phone call in the UK on 1 January from St Katherine's Dock, East London, to Vodafone's HQ in Newbury, Berkshire.

1990

Ernie publishes his memoirs, *Still on my Way to Hollywood*.

1993

Forty Minutes documentary titled "The Importance of Being Ernie". Ernie's life post-Eric, is harshly scrutinised.

1994

Behind the Sunshine by Gary Morecambe and Martin Sterling is published by Robson Books to mark the tenth anniversary of Eric's death.

The BBC mark the same anniversary with Ben Elton introducing a "best of" series. It tops the ratings.

1995

A blue plaque commemorating Eric is put on his former North London home by Comic Heritage, with the unveiling by Victoria Wood.

Ernie announces his retirement aged 70.

1996

Morecambe and Wise are voted the favourite entertainers of all time by a television viewers' poll to mark 60 years of BBC Television.

1998

Radio Times readers vote Morecambe and Wise the best TV comedy stars of all time.

Morecambe and Wise, by Graham McCann, is published
Omnibus: The Heart and Soul of Eric Morecambe is broadcast on BBC1.

1999

Ernie Wise dies, aged 73.

Eric and Ernie are each awarded a posthumous BAFTA fellowship.

A statue of Eric is unveiled in Morecambe Bay, Lancashire by HM the Queen.

Eric and Ernie are honoured with a blue plaque in Pinewood Studios' Hall of Fame to commemorate their three film outings for Rank.

The documentary-style and clips television tribute to Morecambe and Wise, *The Sunshine Boys*, presented by Michael Parkinson, is transmitted.

2000

An Internet poll votes Eric the greatest British comedian of the twentieth century.

2002

Eric is voted no. 32 in an All-time Great Britons poll.
The Play What I Wrote wins two Olivier awards.

2003

The Play What I Wrote opens to positive reviews on Broadway, New York, and is shortlisted for a Tony award.

2009

A Morecambe and Wise image is used on T-shirts designed by Stella McCartney and David Bailey for the Comic Relief Red Nose Appeal.

The one-man play *Morecambe*, starring Bob Golding, opens at the Edinburgh Festival and wins an Olivier award.

2010

A statue of Ernie Wise is unveiled in Morley, Leeds.

Morecambe and Wise: The Garage Tapes, a BBC Radio 4 documentary about archive recordings of the double act, is broadcast.

Victoria Wood develops and starts filming a BBC drama for the festive season called *Eric and Ernie*. It covers their early years, and she portrays Eric's mother Sadie.

2011

Victoria Wood's TV film *Eric and Ernie* is screened. It wins a BAFTA for Daniel Rigby, who plays the grown-up Eric.

2012

UK GOLD acquires rights to make a five-part series, part documentary and clip-based, of Morecambe and Wise called *Bring Me Morecambe and Wise*.

Children In Need create holograms of Morecambe and Wise singing "Bring Me Sunshine" accompanied by radio presenter Chris Moyles.

Gary Morecambe begins work with Bob Golding, who starred in the one-man show *Morecambe*, on turning Eric's novel *Stella* into a touring play.

Left and overleaf Eric and Ernie recreate their famous dance routine outside the gates of Buckingham Palace on the day they received their OBEs and pose with their medals, or in Eric's case, his watch!

Credits

Above Eric and Ernie sign off on another memorable performance.

Picture credits

The publishers would like to thank the following sources for their kind permission to reproduce the pictures in this book

Alamy Images: Juliet Ferguson 11 (top right)

© BBC: 6 (below left), 81, 82 (top right), 83 (top left), 83 (bottom), 88 (top), 91 (bottom left), 100-101, 103 (left), 103 (right), 104 (top left), 66 (bottom left), 105 (bottom), 109, 110 (top left), 113, 114 (bottom), 115, 116

Rex Features Associated Press 82 (bottom); /Courtesy Everett Collection 20 (bottom); /FreemantleMedia Ltd 6 (top left), 83 (top right), 105 (top), 111, 124 (top right), 124 (bottom), 125 (top), 126, 127 (top left), 133, 143; /ITV 55 (bottom)

Getty Images: John Chillingworth 28 (bottom centre); /Hulton Archive 13; /Keystone 55 (top); Lipnitzki/Roger Violett 11 (bottom); Graham Stark 83 (centre); /MacGregor/Topical press Agency 15 (top right); /Popperfoto 51

Mary Evans Picture Library: 28 (bottom right)

© Radio Times: 112, 117

Ronald Grant Archive: ITV Global Entertainment 74 (top left)

Vestry House Museum: 27 (right)

Every effort has been made to acknowledge correctly and contact the source and/or copyright holder of each picture and Carlton Books Limited apologises for any unintentional errors or omissions, which will be corrected in future editions of this book.

Memorabilia credits

Mrs Eric Morecambe: 16, 44-45, 56, 58, 59, 73, 78-79, 84-86, 89-90, 99, 122, 144

Mrs Ernie Wise: 36-37, 64-69, 72, 92, 93-95, 123

Mr Eddie Braben: 106-107